# THE PHILOSOPHY OF KANT

KEY TEXTS
**Classic Studies in the History of Ideas**

# THE PHILOSOPHY OF KANT

## John Kemp

ST. AUGUSTINE'S PRESS
South Bend, Indiana

Reprinted by arrangement with Oxford University Press
© Oxford University Press 1968

Manufactured in the United States of America.

1 2 3 4 5 6  07 06 05 04 03 02 01

Library of Congress Cataloging in Publication Data
Kemp, John, 1920–
    The philosophy of Kant / John Kemp.
      p. cm. – (Key texts (South Bend, Ind.))
    Originally published: London ; New York : Oxford University
    Press, 1968, in series: Oxford paperbacks university series.
    Includes bibliographical references and index.
    ISBN 1-890318-72-8 (alk. paper)
    Kant, Immanuel, 1724–1804. I. Title. II. Series.

B2798.K33 2000
193 – dc21                                  00-062608

∞ *The paper used in this publication meets the minimum requirements of the
American National Standard for Information Sciences – Permanence of
Paper for Printed Materials, ANSI Z39.48-1984.*

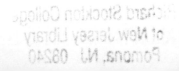

# Contents

# Abbreviations and References

| | |
|---|---|
| *Grundlegung* | *Grundlegung zur Metaphysik der Sitten* (Groundwork, or Fundamental Principles, of the Metaphysic of Morals) |
| KPV | *Kritik der praktischen Vernunft* (Critique of Practical Reason) |
| KRV | *Kritik der reinen Vernunft* (Critique of Pure Reason) |
| KU | *Kritik der Urteilskraft* (Critique of Judgement) |
| MdS | *Die Metaphysik der Sitten* (The Metaphysic of Morals) |
| *Prolegomena* | *Prolegomena zu einer jeden künftigen Metaphysik, die als Wissenschaft wird auftreten können* (Prolegomena to any Future Metaphysic that will be able to present itself as a Science) |
| *Religion* | *Die Religion innerhalb der Grenzen der blossen Vernunft* (Religion within the Bounds of Reason Alone) |

When quoting passages from Kant I have used the following translations, with occasional modifications:

*Critique of Pure Reason*: translated by N. Kemp Smith (Macmillan, London, 1929)

*Critique of Practical Reason*: translated by L. W. Beck (Library of Liberal Arts, New York)

*Critique of Judgement*: (*a*) *First Introduction*: translated by J. Haden (Library of Liberal Arts, New York)

    (*b*) The *Analytic* of the *Critique of Aesthetic Judgement* ('*Analytic of the Beautiful*'): translated by W. Cerf (Library of Liberal Arts, New York)

    (*c*) remainder: translated by J. C. Meredith (Clarendon Press, Oxford, 1952)

*Grundlegung*: translated by H. J. Paton (Hutchinson, London, 1948)

*Prolegomena*: translated by P. G. Lucas (Manchester University Press, 1953)

*Metaphysik der Sitten*: (*a*) Part I, *Metaphysical Elements of Justice*: translated by J. Ladd (Library of Liberal Arts, New York)

    (*b*) Part II, *Metaphysical Elements of Virtue*: translated by Mary J. Gregor (Harper Torchbooks, New York)

*Religion*: translated by T. M. Greene and H. H. Hudson (Harper Torchbooks, New York)

*Lectures on Education*: translated by Annette Churton (Michigan University Press)

*What is Enlightenment?* in *Critique of Practical Reason and Other Writings in Moral Philosophy*: translated by L. W. Beck (Chicago University Press)

Page references to the *Critique of Pure Reason* are given, in the conventional way, to the pages of the first and second editions, which are quoted in the margin of Kemp Smith's translation (e.g. 'A321 B377' means 'page 321 of the first edition and page 377 of the second'). All other references are to the volume and page number of the collected edition of Kant's works published by the Prussian Academy, Berlin. These page numbers are quoted in all except two of the translations referred to, that of the *Analytic* of the *Critique of Aesthetic Judgement* (by Cerf) and that of *Religion within the Bounds of Reason Alone*. When quoting from them I have therefore added a reference to the page of the translation.

# Introduction

THE EXTERNAL CIRCUMSTANCES of Immanuel Kant's life can be simply and briefly described. He was born in the Prussian town of Königsberg (now Kaliningrad) on 22 April 1724. He lived there all his life apart from a brief period which he spent as a young man serving as a tutor, first in the family of the pastor at Judschen (from about 1747 to 1750) and then (from 1750 to 1754) at Gross-Arnsdorf, the estate of the Von Hülsens. He came of a relatively poor family (his father was a harness-maker); there does not seem to be any truth in the story that his paternal grandfather was an immigrant from Scotland, even though Kant himself believed it. His parents belonged to the Pietist movement, a branch of the Lutheran church which valued moral goodness and purity of heart more than dogma and outward forms. In spite of his modest circumstances, he was able to attend the local high school and eventually, in 1740, to enter the University of Königsberg as a student in the faculty of philosophy. After his employment as tutor referred to above, he returned to Königsberg and was appointed in 1755 to the post of *Privatdocent* (private lecturer) in the University. He gave regular courses of lectures, which continued after his appointment in 1770 to the professorship of logic and metaphysics. He gave up lecturing through weakness and ill health in 1799, and died on 12 February 1804.

Kant's lectures and writings cover a great variety of topics. Within philosophy in the narrow sense, he lectured on logic, metaphysics, and moral philosophy; in addition, there was a popular and often repeated course on physical geography, as well as others on anthropology, theoretical physics, and mathematics. His essays and books, especially those of his earlier years, are scarcely less wide-ranging. While a complete and adequate account of Kant's mental life would have to take all this into account, however, this book is concerned with his philosophical work alone; and within this field, a second limit is set on its scope, for a reason which requires explanation. Some great philosophers have done much of their most original and important work early in their lives (Berkeley and Hume come to mind as extreme examples); others show a steady progress of thought from earlier work to later, the earlier not only giving clear indications of what the later developments were to be but also being philosophically important in its own right. Kant falls into neither of these categories. If he had died at the age of fifty-five, he would have been remembered locally as a stimulating and devoted teacher (in contrast to many of his contemporaries) and as the writer of some interesting philosophical essays; but no one would have placed him, as he is now securely placed, among the very greatest philosophers. Moreover, although the writings of his philosophical maturity, beginning with the *Critique of Pure Reason*, which was published in 1781 but on which he had been working for some years, can be shown to be not without their anticipations and preliminary exercises in his earlier work, they do represent a fundamentally new approach to philosophy, and are not the outcome of a steady process of development.[1] The position may be expressed briefly, and perhaps not too misleadingly, by saying that whereas Kant, in what has come to be called his pre-critical period, was prepared for the most part to engage actively in the current philosophical controversies of his day, his later 'critical' writings are aimed, not at contributing to philosophical controversy, but at resolving the disputes and disagreements of both contemporary and traditional philosophy by showing that, although each major position has something to be said for it, all are nevertheless inadequate because they have not inquired deeply enough into the capacity of the human mind for thought and the attainment of truth.

This book, then, attempts an exposition of Kant's mature philosophical thinking.[2] It does not attempt to trace the relation of his critical philosophy to the pre-critical, interesting and valuable though such an exercise might be;[3] nor does it attempt to examine in detail its sources or

[1] See the Note on p. 4.
[2] It does not concern itself with the interpretation of the so-called *Opus Postumum*, a collection of unpublished material written towards the close of Kant's life, in which some scholars have seen signs of a radical departure from some of the principal theses of the critical philosophy, while others again have found in it little but confirmation of them.
[3] The classic work on the development of Kant's philosophical thinking is H.-J. de Vleeschauwer, *La Déduction transcendentale dans l'œuvre de Kant* (Antwerp-Paris-The Hague, 1934-7). A condensed version of this enormous book appeared in 1939, and has been translated into English by A. R. C. Duncan under the title *The Development of Kantian Thought* (London, 1962).

stimuli in the philosophy of Kant's contemporaries and immediate pre-decessors.[1] Even with these limitations, the exposition is necessarily selective. The decision whether to discuss one topic and to ignore another, or to discuss one at length and another briefly, is one with which the writer of any short text on a great and prolific thinker is continually faced. Moreover, there are many places in Kant's work, especially perhaps in the *Critique of Pure Reason*, where the interpretation of what he says is still a matter of intense controversy among scholars. It is impossible in a work of this scope to argue at length for and against different interpretations; and the reader may be left on occasion with the natural but erroneous impression that, whatever one may think as to the truth of what Kant says, there can be no doubt as to what he meant. It cannot be too emphatically stressed, therefore, that in its selection of what is to be expounded, in the relative space which it devotes to different topics, and in its interpretation of difficult and disputed passages, this book represents merely the judgement and opinion of one student of Kant and that that judgement and opinion might well be challenged, and quite legitimately challenged, on almost every point. There is no question of attempting an authoritative exposition of Kant, whatever that might be; and if anyone wishes to understand Kant there is no substitute for reading him. The most that one can hope for is that an exposition of this kind may make the reading of Kant a little easier; but it will not make it easy, for Kant is often an extremely difficult writer (perhaps the most difficult of all the great philosophers). This difficulty is due, not primarily to any deficiencies in Kant's literary style—his writing is sometimes careless, but the carelessness itself rarely causes difficulty to the careful reader—but to the extreme difficulty of the questions with which he is attempting to deal and to the fact that, as a pioneer in this kind of philosophical thinking, he has to develop his own style and terminology as he goes along. (When he is writing, whether early or late in life, on less difficult and abstruse topics, his style is more often than not admirably clear.) The primary object of this book, then, is expository; such criticism and assessment as it contains are subordinate to this main object. Many of Kant's views and arguments are, of course, open to criticism; but he has, more perhaps than most, suffered from the reluctance of philosophers to believe that one should try hard to understand a man's thought before deciding what is wrong with it; the most valuable

[1] A useful account for the English reader of some relevant contemporary German philosophy, especially that of Wolff, Baumgarten, and Meier, is to be found in T. D. Weldon, *Kant's Critique of Pure Reason* (2nd edn. Oxford, 1958).

criticism of a great philosopher will come from within, as it were, after
the critic has mastered his thought and made it his own, not from an
external and superficial attitude.

## NOTE

The publication dates of some of Kant's most important works are
given below:

1755   *Universal Natural History and Theory of the Heavens*
1763   *The Only Possible Ground for a Demonstration of the Existence
       of God*
1764   *Observations on the Feeling of the Beautiful and the Sublime*
1766   *Dreams of a Spirit-Seer*
1770   Inaugural lecture: *Dissertation on the Form and Principles of the
       Sensible and Intelligible World*
1781   *Critique of Pure Reason* (First edition)
1783   *Prolegomena to any Future Metaphysic that will be able to present
       itself as a Science*
1785   *Groundwork, or Fundamental Principles, of the Metaphysic of
       Morals*
1786   *Metaphysical First Principles of Natural Science*
1787   *Critique of Pure Reason* (Second edition)
1788   *Critique of Practical Reason*
1790   *Critique of Judgement*
1792-3 *Religion within the Bounds of Reason Alone*
1797   *Metaphysic of Morals*
1798   *Anthropology from a Practical Point of View*

# 1
# The Conditions of Knowledge

KANT'S THOUGHT, even if we consider the *Critique of Pure Reason* alone, ranges over a great variety of topics and includes arguments of widely differing types and degrees of significance. There are, for example, important contributions (important whether we now find them acceptable or not) to the philosophy of mathematics and the philosophy of science; and these and other similar contributions are developed to a depth and a length which, although it may be commensurate with their intrinsic value, is not always easy to relate to any central argument or thesis of the *Critique*, taken as a whole. Yet there is at the back of the *Critique* a central problem and a central thesis which forms an essential part of the solution to this problem, even though, in Kant's view, it solves other, less central, problems as well. (The direction of thought is more clearly seen in the *Prolegomena*, where his system is presented in outline with expository clarity as the main aim; in the *Critiques*, on the other hand, and especially in the *Critique of Pure Reason*, the objective is rigorous proof and the order of events is determined by this objective without regard to the convenience of the reader who wants to understand the general trend of what is going on.) Kant's central problem, in fact, concerns the status of metaphysics: all previous metaphysical thinking can be shown to have involved itself in uncertainties and contradictions, and these must be resolved if metaphysics is ever to become a genuine science, fit to rank with mathematics or physics.

Metaphysics is thought of by Kant as the philosophical inquiry into first principles which is categorized, in accordance with contemporary practice, under three heads, God, freedom, and immortality; it is the investigation by rational methods of the nature and attributes of God, the existence and presuppositions of human freedom (free will), and the immortality of the human soul. Since the time of Plato, and even earlier, down to Kant's own day, philosophers had tried to discover conclusive proofs and demonstrations in these matters—that God exists, that He has such-and-such attributes and powers, that man possesses free will, that he possesses a soul which will continue to exist after the end of his present earthly life. But whereas in other branches of fundamental systematic thinking (*Wissenschaft* or science in the wide sense of the word), mathematics and physics for example, general agreement and certainty has in many respects been reached, this is not true of metaphysics. Disagreement and controversy are as prevalent now as they were in the days of Plato and Aristotle; arguments which convince one set of thinkers are thought by others to lack all cogency. Because of this, metaphysics has in the eyes of many lost her early reputation as queen of the sciences.

The principal errors into which metaphysics has fallen are divided by Kant into three groups. Some appear in the branch of metaphysics known as rational psychology, which is the attempt to discover truths about the nature of the soul by philosophical reflection, as contrasted with an empirical investigation into associated phenomena; others in rational theology, which is the attempt to discover proofs of the existence of God and truths about His nature, again by philosophical reasoning, as opposed to empirical investigation or divine revelation. But although Kant attached importance to errors in these two branches of metaphysics, they do not seem to have provided much stimulus for his fundamentally critical attitude to all existing metaphysics; fallacious or otherwise unsatisfactory attempts to prove the immortality of the soul or the existence of God can be refuted, he thought, without casting doubt on the whole metaphysical enterprise (this is mainly due to the fact that no metaphysicians attempt to prove the mortality of the soul or the non-existence of God). But with the third branch of metaphysics, rational cosmology, the situation is different; here conflicting arguments appear within metaphysics and yet, on the ordinary metaphysical assumptions, both sets of conflicting arguments appear to be equally valid. The resulting contradictions, or antinomies as Kant calls them, are in a sense inherent in reason itself; they can be resolved (indeed, the entire *Critique of Pure Reason* can be regarded as an attempt to resolve them), but a long and roundabout course of philosophical thinking is necessary before the resolution can take place.

Detailed discussion of Kant's treatment of the antinomies must for the moment be postponed; but it may be as well to list them at this stage. They are four in number, and the contradictions they contain are systematic, supporting dogmatic or sceptical tendencies according as one member or the other of each pair of conflicting theses is espoused.

1. *Thesis*: The world has a beginning in time and is limited as regards space.
*Antithesis*: The world is infinite in both time and space.

2. *Thesis*: Every composite substance in the world is made up of simple parts, and nothing anywhere exists save the simple or what is composed of the simple.
*Antithesis*: No composite thing in the world is made up of simple parts, and there nowhere exists anything simple.

3. *Thesis*: Causality in accordance with laws of nature is not the only causality from which the appearances of the world can one and all be derived. To explain these appearances it is necessary to assume that there is also a causality of freedom.
*Antithesis*: There is no freedom; everything in the world takes place solely in accordance with laws of nature.

4. *Thesis*: There belongs to the world, either as its part or as its cause, a being that is absolutely necessary.
*Antithesis*: An absolutely necessary being does not exist in the world, nor does it exist outside the world as its cause.

Since these contradictions occur in the course of reasoning, and since they seem to be so deeply entrenched in the activity of reasoning itself, Kant takes the view that the whole of metaphysics rests on shaky founda- tions, and that it will continue to do so until a full inquiry into the work- ing of reason itself has been undertaken. He proposes, then, to substitute a critical approach for a dogmatic one; instead of dogmatically assuming, as previous writers on metaphysics have done, that our intellectual powers are sufficient for the making of the discoveries which are the object of metaphysics, he insists that metaphysical investigation be suspended until a full inquiry has been made into the nature of our reasoning powers and their suitability for this metaphysical task.[1] Kant

---

[1] Kant had himself been guilty, in his earlier thinking, of some metaphysical errors of the type which he is now criticizing; in 1763, for example, he published an essay entitled *The Only Possible Ground for a Demonstration of the Existence of God*, containing a defence of a method of theological argument, from analysis of concepts to an existential conclusion, which he later came to regard as inadequate. Even though he had always considered the frequent conflicts between philosophers as a reproach or scandal, he had not at first made any systematic attempt to see how the conflicts could be resolved; and between the undertaking of this attempt (in about 1770, as we know from his letters) and the publication of the first edition of the *Critique* eleven years had elapsed—hardly surprising when we consider the magnitude of the undertaking.

was not, of course, the first to suggest the desirability of reflection of this general kind. Descartes' method of pretending to doubt everything that could be doubted without absurdity, leading to his conclusion that he could not possibly doubt his own existence as a thinking being, and to the erection on this foundation of a whole system of knowledge, marks at least a small advance on the completely unreflective attitudes of his predecessors to the mental apparatus with which metaphysical discoveries were supposed to be made; but Descartes stops well short of a systematic investigation of the kind which Kant demands, and makes more assumptions than his method, if strictly observed, would entitle him to. Locke might be thought to have provided something much nearer the mark; for in writing the *Essay concerning Human Understanding* he set out to examine the operation of the human mind in the hope that he might thereby discover which are the matters on which we may hope to attain certainty and which are those in which we must remain content with opinion and conjecture. But Locke's 'physiology of the human understanding', as Kant calls it (KRV Aix), is in his view quite inadequate to serve its intended purpose; it does not probe deeply enough and remains limited by its empirical approach.

> The illustrious Locke, failing to take account of these considerations [sc. the need to validate the pure concepts of the understanding as a priori conditions of the possibility of experience], and meeting with pure concepts of the understanding in experience, deduced them also from experience, and yet proceeded so inconsequently that he attempted with their aid to obtain knowledge which far transcends all limits of experience. (KRV B127.)

The only one of Kant's predecessors to whom he is prepared to give credit for making a serious contribution to the problem is David Hume. Hume was the first to expose in a serious philosophical way the difficulties which must be faced by any attempt to achieve results in metaphysics, and Kant acknowledged his work, in a famous phrase, as having first woken him from his dogmatic slumbers.[1] His main contribution to this awakening concerned his treatment of the relation of cause and effect, and he showed that reason alone, working a priori from concepts, cannot demonstrate that any particular effect must necessarily result from a given cause; the cause–effect relationship is discovered in experience.

---

[1] Elsewhere, in his letters, Kant attributes his awakening to his reflections on the antinomies. There is, however, no real contradiction here; what impressed Kant was the effect which Hume's sceptical conclusions, and especially the general implications of his treatment of the concept of cause, would have on the whole status of metaphysics, considered as a possible systematic body of knowledge.

As Kant puts it (*Prol.* IV 257), 'The imagination, having by experience brought certain representations under the law of association, passes off a subjective necessity arising out of this, namely custom, for an objective necessity from insight.' Reason, then, cannot, in Hume's view, establish a priori connexions; and to illustrate the general implications of this thesis Kant might well have quoted the famous concluding paragraph of the *Inquiry concerning Human Understanding*:

When we run over libraries, persuaded of these principles, what havoc must we make? If we take in our hand any volume—of divinity or school metaphysics, for example—let us ask, *Does it contain any abstract reasoning concerning quantity or number?* No. *Does it contain any experimental reasoning concerning matter of fact and existence?* No. Commit it then to the flames, for it can contain nothing but sophistry and illusion. (XII. iii.)

In arriving at this sceptical conclusion, Kant thought, Hume was at least consistent, unlike Locke; if our concepts are derived from experience we cannot use them to transcend experience. But Hume's thinking was nevertheless defective. In the first place it was insufficiently generalized, since it dealt with the concepts of cause and effect only, and took no account of the other pure concepts of the understanding. Secondly, it stopped short in a sceptical position about the capacities of reason; having decided what reason could not do, it failed to take the next step of asking what reason can do. (Hume had to some extent done this in the *Treatise of Human Nature*, unknown to Kant;[1] but even if he had known this, it would not have caused him to alter his judgement: 'He draws no distinction between the well-grounded claims of the understanding and the dialectical pretensions of reason, though it is indeed chiefly against the latter that his attacks are directed' (KRV A768 B796).) Thirdly, and more specifically, Hume failed properly to distinguish questions about the origin or justification of a belief that X caused Y from questions about the origin or justification of a belief that, whatever caused Y, it must have had *some* cause; in Kant's view, experience is necessary to know what caused any change to take place, but we know a priori (i.e. independently of experience) that something must have caused it.

Kant's attempts to remedy these deficiencies of Hume's philosophy

---

[1] Kant's knowledge of the relevant work of Hume was limited to the *Inquiry*, and to those few passages of the *Treatise* which had been quoted by James Beattie in his *Essay on the Nature and Immutability of Truth*. Unlike the *Inquiry* and the *Essay*, the *Treatise* had not at this time been translated into German, and Kant did not read English.

while retaining the essence of his insight into the problem are described
in a passage of the *Prolegomena* which is worth quoting at some length.

So I first tried whether Hume's objection could not be represented universally,
and I soon found that the concept of the connection of cause and effect is by no
means the only one by which connections between things are thought a priori by
the understanding; indeed that metaphysics consists of nothing else whatever.
I tried to make certain of the number of these concepts, and when I had succeeded
in doing this in the way I wished, namely from a single principle, I proceeded to
the deduction of them. I was now assured that they are not, as Hume has feared,
deduced from experience, but have their origin in pure understanding. This
deduction, which seemed impossible to my sagacious predecessor, and had never
even occurred to anyone except him, although everyone confidently used these
concepts without asking on what their objective validity is grounded—this
deduction, I say, was the most difficult thing that could ever be undertaken on
behalf of metaphysics; and, worst of all, any metaphysics that there is anywhere
at all could not give me the slightest help, because this deduction has first to establish the possibility of a metaphysics. Having succeeded in solving Hume's
problem not merely in a special case, but with regard to the whole faculty of pure
reason, I could take sure although still only slow steps towards determining at
last the whole extent of pure reason, completely and according to universal
principles, in its boundaries as well as in its content. This is what metaphysics
needs in order to construct its system according to a sure plan. (*Prol.* IV 260.)

It is no use relying, as some of Hume's critics tried to do, on an appeal
to common sense as a corrective to his sceptical and paradoxical conclusions. The value of common sense is confined to the making of judgements based on sense-experience, and it can contribute nothing to the
discovery of universal a priori truths, which is the business of metaphysics. A thoroughgoing philosophical proof that we have a right to
use such fundamental concepts as cause and substance must be provided
if the hope of obtaining results from our metaphysical thinking is to be
more than an illusion. This proof (or 'deduction', in a rather special sense
of the word) is in a way the central feature of the *Critique of Pure Reason*;
but other features require consideration before we can usefully discuss
it in detail.

Given, then, that the first step in the assessment of the claims of metaphysicians to have a knowledge of fundamental truths which is derived
from reasoning alone is to examine the nature and structure of our reasoning powers, what form is this examination to take? It is clear that metaphysical knowledge, if there is such a thing, is not a kind of empirical
knowledge. We do not discover that there is a God, or that the soul is
immortal, or that man possesses free will, by sensory observation; we

cannot see, hear, or touch God, nor observe an immortal soul, nor can we observe a man's will operating freely (we can observe behaviour which we take, rightly or wrongly, to be the effect of the free operation of a man's will, but this is not the same thing).

Metaphysical knowledge, then, if it exists, is a priori knowledge. Now there are three sciences which yield a priori knowledge, logic, mathematics, and physics; it may therefore be helpful, Kant suggests, to try to discover what it is that enables these inquiries to deserve the name of science.[1] Kant's answer to this question, to anticipate, is that they use a priori judgements in a way that can be philosophically justified, even if philosophers have not as yet given an entirely satisfactory justification of it. Logic, however, is a special case; for its principles, though a priori, are analytic, and can therefore be derived or justified quite simply from the law of contradiction. Mathematics and physics, however, yield synthetic (as opposed to analytic) a priori knowledge;[2] and since this is what metaphysics also would have to do if it were to yield any knowledge at all, the possibility of acquiring synthetic a priori knowledge of the required type may turn out to be a necessary condition of the possibility of any science. What happens, in fact, in the main body of the *Critique* is that Kant first (in the sections entitled 'Transcendental Aesthetic' and 'Transcendental Analytic') explains just how the possibility of synthetic a priori judgements enables us to establish the sciences of mathematics and physics on a firm foundation; subsequently (in the section entitled 'Transcendental Dialectic') he argues that, since theoretical reason cannot make valid synthetic a priori judgements which refer to objects outside the bounds of possible sense-experience, the traditional attempts of speculative metaphysics to solve the problems of God, freedom, and immortality are bound to fail. The synthetic a priori judgements of mathematics, although they do not describe our actual sense-experience —if they did they would not be a priori—do nevertheless refer to objects

---

[1] Kant takes it for granted that logic, mathematics, and physics are genuine sciences, but he explains very clearly why he thinks that metaphysics, as at present practised, is not:

'Whether the treatment of such knowledge as lies within the province of reason does or does not follow the secure path of a science, is easily to be determined from the outcome. For if after elaborate preparations, frequently renewed, it is brought to a stop immediately it nears its goal; if often it is compelled to retrace its steps and strike into some new line of approach; or again, if the various participants are unable to agree in any common plan of procedure, then we may rest assured that it is very far from having entered upon the secure path of a science, and is indeed a merely random groping.' (KRV Bvii.)

[2] Physics contains empirical statements, of course, but it rests on fundamental a priori principles (basic laws of motion, for example, and the principle of conservation of energy).

of possible experience and therefore escape the objections brought against speculative metaphysics.

We must now explain in some detail the two technical distinctions which have played an important part in this outline statement of Kant's problem and his attempted solution, that between empirical and a priori (or, more strictly, between a posteriori and a priori), and that between analytic and synthetic.

Kant's use of the first of these distinctions is comparatively straight-forward, although it differs in some respects from that now current among philosophers. Empirical knowledge is that obtained from experience, a priori knowledge that which is obtained independently of experience. The nature and structure of experience, and the respective parts played in it by sensation and thought are, as we shall see, topics on which Kant has important and controversial things to say, but the basic distinction is uncomplicated. I know from experience (i.e. a posteriori, empirically) that the turning of water into ice is caused by a reduction in temperature to 0° Centigrade or less; I could not know this unless I, or someone on whose trustworthiness I can rely, had made certain relevant observations, and unless similar observations and correlations between observations could be made now or in the future. But I know a priori, in Kant's view, that the turning of water into ice must have *some* cause, even though experience is necessary before I can know what its cause is; speaking generally, I do not have to discover empirically that events have causes, for I can know this even in advance of any experience.[1] Now there could, of course, be differences of degree in the use of a phrase such as 'dependent on experience'. We could say that if a man has under-mined the foundations of his house, he might have known a priori that it would collapse, without having to wait until he saw the collapse with his own eyes; but this would be a loose use of 'a priori', since the man could know that the house would collapse only if he knew some general truth such that unsupported bodies tend to fall, and this he could know only from experience. Kant therefore confines his serious use of the phrase to a stricter type of case in which the knowledge is, as he puts it, absolutely independent of all experience; further, within this category he dis-tinguishes pure a priori knowledge as being knowledge the content of

---

[1] The temporal suggestion of the phrases 'a priori' and 'a posteriori' and of some of Kant's language when he is discussing this topic is not to be taken literally. The question is not one of genetic psychology; i.e. it is not a question of what one has been doing or what has been happening before one's knowledge is acquired, but of the need, or otherwise, to *rely* on experience for one's knowledge.

which includes nothing at all that is empirical. We can know a priori that every alteration has a cause, but this is not *pure* a priori knowledge, because the concept of alteration itself is derived from experience, even though, once that concept is formed, our knowledge that anything which falls under it has a cause is independent of experience. Our knowledge, on the other hand, that if $a = b$ and $b = c$ then $a = c$ is pure a priori knowledge.

The analytic–synthetic distinction, by contrast, is Kant's own, although rather less systematic anticipations of it are found in some earlier writers. It plays an even more important part in Kant's philosophy than the empirical–a priori distinction, and needs a good deal of elucidation. It is particularly necessary to avoid the mistake of supposing that Kant's use of the distinction is identical with that, or those, current among twentieth-century philosophers. The first thing to be noticed is that the distinction is, for Kant, primarily a distinction between judgements, although he also applies it frequently to propositions; and his concentration on judgements and the act of judging explains why he defines 'analytic' and 'synthetic' in terms of what is thought or judged in the act of thinking a certain concept rather than in terms of what is asserted, for example, in saying that a subject possesses a certain attribute. Another important feature is that his detailed account of the distinction is explicitly limited in its application to the class of affirmative categorical judgements, i.e. to judgements which make an unconditional assertion; he says that it is easy to make the amendments necessary to apply the distinction to negative judgements, and its application to hypothetical judgements, i.e. to judgements of the 'If . . . then . . .' form which assert a relation of ground to consequent, though he does not discuss it at any length, does not seem to present much of a problem.

If we take a simple subject–predicate judgement, Kant says, the relation between subject and predicate may be thought of in one of two ways. Either the predicate is (covertly or overtly) contained in the concept of the subject, or the predicate stands outside the subject-concept, even though it is of course connected with it. In the former case the judgement is analytic, in the latter it is synthetic. In 'All men are men' the predicate is overtly contained in, or rather, identical with, the subject-concept; such judgements Kant calls tautologous, and he regards them as useless. The judgement 'All Greek men are men', in which the predicate is overtly contained in, though not identical with, the subject-concept, is not strictly tautologous in Kant's sense, but is presumably just as useless. But in 'All bodies are extended' the predicate is covertly contained in the subject–concept, i.e. the relation is implicit, not explicit; and analytic judgements of this kind are by no means useless, for they can have explanatory and clarificatory value—they can elucidate a concept by pointing out another concept which is included in it. 'All bodies are heavy', on the other hand, is synthetic; for although the concept of heaviness is connected with the concept of body, it is not contained in it. In the synthetic judgement, two different concepts are being combined in thought (hence the name 'synthetic'): in the analytic judgement, on the other hand, we have a concept to the left, as it were, of the copula and either the same concept or, more usually, a part of it, to the right. A synthetic judgement can clearly add to our knowledge; for the connexion between the subject and the predicate is something that we could not have discovered from the analysis of the subject–concept alone.

Now this notion of one concept being contained in another, which is at the basis of Kant's distinction between analytic and synthetic judgements, is not perhaps as clear as it might be. It has a metaphorical air about it which seems out of place in a logical context. Kant, however, does say enough in elucidation of it for us to be able to grasp its general outline, at least, satisfactorily enough. Especially important is the connexion between the analytic-synthetic distinction and the law of contradiction. This law, Kant repeatedly says, is the principle of analytic judgements; and by this he means that when a true judgement is analytic the denial that the predicate belongs to the subject involves a breach of the law of contradiction. When 'S is P' is analytic, 'S is not P' entails 'S is not S', and is thus self-contradictory. Kant's reason for holding this is simple enough; if 'S is P' is analytic, then in thinking S I am *eo ipso* thinking P, and so to deny P of S is to deny S of itself. It has sometimes been objected that this reference to what I am thinking in making a judgement constitutes an illegitimate intrusion of psychological factors into logic; but this objection is not well founded. It is true that Kant sometimes explains the statement that 'All bodies are extended' is analytic by saying that in thinking of something as a body I am thinking of it as (among other things) extended; but the resemblance between this explanation and a psychological statement such as 'Whenever I think of England I think of green fields' is superficial and misleading. Kant's point is not that whenever anyone thinks of a thing as being a body he must also, by association of ideas, think of it as being extended—this *would* be psychological—but that whenever anyone thinks of a thing as being a body he is thereby thinking of it as being extended. The word 'body' stands for what Kant calls a manifold or multiplicity, and extension is one of the aspects of that manifold to which I refer whenever I thinkingly use the word 'body' in making a judgement. Even though I am not necessarily conscious of this aspect of the manifold on every occasion on which I use the word, I become conscious of it in analysing the concept, i.e. in reflecting on the manifold which I always think in that concept.

It is still, however, not entirely clear how Kant would deal with someone who maintained either that 'All bodies are heavy' is analytic or that 'All bodies are extended' is not. Mere reference to the law of contradiction will not necessarily suffice; for the concepts of analyticity and contradiction are so closely bound up with each other that someone who denied that 'All bodies are extended' is analytic would presumably also deny that 'Some bodies are not extended' is self-contradictory. Now where the subject-term of a judgement is one which has been more or less officially defined, it will be comparatively easy to decide, on Kantian principles, whether the judgement is analytic or not; if a physicist or a metaphysician defines 'body' in such a way that 'All bodies are extended' is true by definition, then the denial that all bodies are extended will violate the law of contradiction, as long as the word 'bodies' is being used in the strictly defined sense, and the judgement will therefore be analytic. But where no such definition is provided, as with any non-technical use of language, there may be room for doubts and arguments as to whether a given judgement is analytic or synthetic. This, however, can hardly be put forward as an objection to Kant, since on any conceivable criterion of analyticity some ordinary non-technical judgements will be difficult to classify. In any case, Kant's main interest is in classifying as analytic or synthetic the judgements which are characteristic of the various sciences or supposed sciences (especially logic, mathematics, physics, and metaphysics); and it is part of the concept of a science that its terms should be univocal and precise. If one tries to answer the question 'Is "All bodies are heavy" analytic or synthetic?' by inquiring into the way in which the word 'body' is used in ordinary, non-technical language, one will not obtain a clear answer in terms of the Kantian distinction; but the difficulty is, to say the least, considerably eased when the question is interpreted by reference to an 'official' definition of body. It is worth remembering in this context that throughout his criticism of speculative metaphysics Kant is working in the more or less technical terminology of Leibniz and his followers, as that of the prevailing doctrine.

Now that these preliminary explanations are concluded, we are in a position to examine Kant's analysis of human knowledge and its conditions. Human knowledge arises through the joint functioning of sensibility and intellect, or understanding; it consists of a union of intuition[1] (the product of sensibility) and concept (the product of the understanding). Sensibility is a passive receptivity, the power of receiving representations of the objects by which it is affected: understanding is an active spontaneity, the power of exercising thought over the objects given us in sensible intuition. Neither by itself can give us knowledge: 'Thoughts without content are empty,' Kant says in a famous phrase (KRV A51 B75), 'intuitions without concepts are blind.' Nevertheless it is possible up to a point—indeed, it is necessary—to consider their functions separately, and this Kant does in the sections of the *Critique of Pure Reason* entitled 'Transcendental Aesthetic' (from the Greek aisthesis = sensation) and 'Transcendental Logic' respectively.

In discussing sensibility, however, Kant is not concerned to give an empirical, psychological account of the way in which the senses actually work (he does this in his lectures on Anthropology); he is interested rather in the principles according to which the material supplied to our sensibility by the senses, whatever this material may be, is necessarily ordered —in the structure of sensation, not its content. Moreover, he is not in the Aesthetic discussing the structure of sense-experience as a whole, which involves the understanding with its formation and use of concepts as well as sensibility; sensibility is initially considered in abstraction from understanding even though, Kant insists, it cannot provide knowledge in isolation—for me to know that the object before me is a house, I must have acquired or formed the concept of a house, and the formation of concepts is the business of the understanding.

In the transcendental aesthetic we shall, therefore, first *isolate* sensibility, by taking away from it everything which the understanding thinks through its concepts, so that nothing may be left save empirical intuition. Secondly, we shall also separate off from it everything which belongs to sensation, so that nothing may remain save pure intuition and the mere form of appearances, which is all that sensibility can supply *a priori*. (KRV A22 B36.)

When these two acts of isolation have been performed, it can be seen that there are two pure forms of sensible intuition; two frameworks, as one might say, in which our actual sensations occur, namely space and time, corresponding to what Kant calls outer and inner sense respectively.

---

[1] *Anschauung* means 'immediate apprehension'; the word is sometimes translated 'perception', but this is liable to lead to confusion with *Wahrnehmung* (sense-perception). Intuition may be either through the senses or 'pure' (the nature of this latter kind will appear shortly).

Kant's first point about space is that it is not an empirical concept derived from our experience of things outside us. We discover empirically, by sensory observation, that a certain object is to the left of, or above, or further from us than, another object; but that objects in general are in spatial relations of some kind to one another is not an empirical generalization from specific spatial statements. For the very discovery that X is to the left of Y already presupposes that we have some 'idea' of space in general. If someone asks us 'What are the spatial relationships between X and Y?' we can, in principle at least, provide an answer from the results of observation. But if someone asks us 'Is X in *any* spatial relationship to Y?' it would be absurd to try to answer this question by making observations; for if the answer was No, this would be conclusive proof that observations made through our senses could not possibly be relevant, and that X and Y (or one of them at least) were not located in space at all. Similarly, we cannot, Kant says, imagine or represent to ourselves the absence or non-existence of space, although we can think of space as being empty of objects. And (although Kant does not make this point explicitly) since we cannot form an idea of a spaceless world, our knowledge that the world is spatial cannot have come to us through sense-experience; we can only observe that S is P if we have some idea of what it would be like for S not to be P. Our apprehension of space, then, is not empirical. But space is not a general concept either. For when we have a general concept there are, or may be, particular objects falling under the concept (as particular houses or triangles fall under the general concept of house or triangle); but there are no particular spaces falling under the general concept of space—there can only be one, all-embracing, space, and if we use the expression 'diverse spaces' we can legitimately mean only various parts of this one space. Our apprehension of space is thus not only not empirical; it is not conceptual or discursive either.

Our apprehension of space is, in fact, based on intuition; but on pure, or a priori, intuition, not empirical intuition. This amounts to saying that spatial experience is a function of the human sensibility; our capacity for receiving sensations from objects outside us is so ordered that these objects are always perceived by us as extended in space. Space, then, is 'nothing but the form of all appearances of outer sense'; and 'it is, therefore, solely from the human standpoint that we can speak of space, of extended things, etc.' (KRV A26 B42). There may, for all we know, be thinking beings whose intuitions are not limited in this way; thus space is a necessary condition of all outer objects as they appear to us, but does not necessarily underlie things as they are in themselves.

Kant's view of time is in many ways analogous to his view of space. We cannot have formed the concept of time from our observation or experience of events happening successively or simultaneously, for the notions of succession and simultaneity themselves presuppose time; succession and simultaneity are temporal concepts and we must therefore already have the concept of time before we can talk about, or grasp the existence of, successive or simultaneous events. Time, again, is not a general concept; for even though we can talk about different times, they are not different instances of one concept (as three words on a page are three different instances of the concept 'word') but different parts of one and the same time.

Time, then, is, like space, an a priori form of intuition; but unlike space, it is a form of our intuition or perception of ourselves and of our inner state, not of our intuition of objects outside us. A further distinction follows: time is a necessary formal condition of all appearances whatsoever—all objects outside us appear to us as extended in space, but all representations whatsoever, whether of inner states or of outer objects, appear to us as succeeding, or simultaneous with, one another in time. 'Just as I can say a priori that all outer appearances are in space, and are determined a priori in conformity with the relations of space, I can also say, from the principle of inner sense, that all appearances whatsoever, that is, all objects of the senses, are in time, and necessarily stand in time-relations' (KRV A34 B51). We cannot say that things as they are in themselves exist in time, any more than we can say that they are spatially extended; but all things as they appear to us in our human condition are in time-relations. Our capacity for receiving sensations, then, is so constructed that whatever its material, it is inevitably arranged in a temporal order and, as far as objects outside us are concerned, in a spatial order as well.

The distinction, so far briefly referred to, between appearances and things in themselves, or, more strictly, between things as they appear to us and things as they are in themselves, is one of the fundamental points in Kant's critical philosophy; but a fuller discussion of it will best be postponed until we have considered the way in which it is applied in Kant's treatment of the categories (the basic concepts by which our experience is structured and organized and which are roughly to the understanding what time and space are to sensibility).

The Transcendental Aesthetic examined the contribution made to our a priori knowledge by the nature and structure of human sensibility:

the enormously long section of the *Critique* entitled 'Transcendental Logic' performs a similar task in respect of the understanding. Transcendental logic thus has a more restricted field than general logic, whose laws relate to empirical judgements and the relations between them as well as to a priori judgements; transcendental logic is concerned only with a sub-class of the a priori, 'with the laws of understanding and reason solely in so far as they relate *a priori* to objects' (KRV A57 B82). General logic lays down certain formal laws (e.g. the laws of contradiction and excluded middle) to which all thinking must conform, but which can never give us any positive criterion of truth or knowledge of objects; a judgement can conform to all the laws of logic and still be untrue. General logic performs its work by analysing the whole formal procedure of understanding and reason into its elements, and this aspect of general logic may therefore, Kant suggests, be called by the noun 'analytic'. Some philosophers, however, have made the mistake of trying to use the laws of logic as positive criteria of truth (as if they could yield a sufficient, not merely a necessary, condition of the truth of a judgement);[1] and when general logic is treated in this way, it can be called dialectic, and is a logic of illusion, not of truth. Kant proceeds to draw an analogous distinction within transcendental logic. The section of the *Critique* entitled 'Transcendental Analytic' establishes the contribution our intellects make to our acquisition of a priori knowledge, and that entitled 'Transcendental Dialectic' is a criticism of the illusions generated by the attempt to make the intellect work in regions and in ways that lie beyond its powers—of the illusions of speculative metaphysics, in fact. But the division is more systematic than this. The human intellect (i.e. the non-sensuous part of the mind) has three faculties or fields of operation, understanding (*Verstand*), judgement (*Urteilskraft*), and reason (*Vernunft*). General logic deals with the respective functions of these faculties, the formation of concepts, judgements, and inferences (i.e. relations between judgements). Transcendental logic, on the other hand, confined as it is to the content of pure a priori knowledge, has a somewhat different division, for the transcendental employment of reason is objectively invalid, and its treatment therefore belongs to the Transcendental Dialectic, not to the Analytic. This latter deals only with the faculties of understanding and judgement, which are the only faculties of the mind that can yield knowledge (although even they require the co-operation of sensibility). The understanding is discussed in Book I

---

[1] Kant is here thinking especially of the use made by Leibniz and his followers of the principle of sufficient reason.

of the 'Transcendental Analytic' (entitled 'Analytic of Concepts'), the judgement in Book II (entitled 'Analytic of Principles, or Doctrine of Judgement').

## Analytic of Concepts

This does not mean analysis of concepts, but an analysis of the faculty of understanding itself, as a means of investigating the possibility of a priori concepts. But since any concept is the predicate of a possible judgement, we can give a systematic and complete account of the pure concepts which are the especial functions of the understanding by giving a systematic and exhaustive statement of the logical forms or types of judgement. As Kant puts it, the purely logical classification of judgements provides a clue to the discovery of all pure concepts of the understanding (or categories).

If we consider the mere form of understanding in abstraction from all content of any actual judgement, we find, according to Kant, that the function of thought in judgement can be classified under four heads, Quantity, Quality, Relation, and Modality; and each of these four classes contains three 'moments' or sub-classes. Under the heading 'Quantity' we may classify judgements as Universal (All men are mortal), Particular (Some men are long-lived), or Singular (Socrates is mortal). Under the heading 'Quality', judgements are either Affirmative (The soul is mortal), Negative (The soul is not mortal), or Infinite (The soul is non-mortal).[1] Under the heading 'Relation' judgements are either Categorical (asserting a relation between two concepts in a subject-predicate judgement—e.g. The wicked are punished), Hypothetical (asserting a relation of ground to consequent between two judgements —e.g. If there is a perfect justice, the wicked are punished), or Disjunctive (asserting a relation of disjunction between two or more judgements—e.g. The world exists either through blind chance, or through inner necessity, or through an external cause—one of these three judgements is true, but not more than one). Finally, under the heading 'Modality', judgements are either Problematic (The cat may be on the mat), Assertoric (The cat is on the mat), or Apodeictic (The cat must be somewhere). According to Kant, this classification is, with some comparatively unimportant modifications, that ordinarily recognized by logicians; and although he stresses the importance of establishing its accuracy and completeness, he does little in fact to show that the

[1] 'Infinite' because the soul is asserted to belong to an infinite or unlimited class of which no more is said than that it does not include the class of things that are mortal.

classification is exhaustive, or even that it is correct as far as it goes. But assuming that we accept its completeness and accuracy, how can we derive from this classification, belonging as it does to general logic, an accurate and exhaustive list of the pure concepts of the understanding? It is done, according to Kant, simply by making use of our knowledge of the essential differences between general and transcendental logic.

General logic, as has been repeatedly said, abstracts from all content of knowledge, and looks to some other source, whatever that may be, for the representations which it is to transform into concepts by process of analysis. Transcendental logic, on the other hand, has lying before it a manifold of *a priori* sensibility, presented by transcendental aesthetic, as material for the concepts of pure understanding. (KRV A76-77 B102.)

Space and time are conditions under which all our ideas or representations of objects are received, and consequently conditions which affect our concepts of those objects. Space and time also contain what Kant calls a manifold of pure a priori intuition—i.e. the fact that the material presented to our understanding is presented under spatial and temporal conditions does not of itself provide us with any means of understanding, or any source of knowledge about, this material; it is at this stage an unstructured manifold or multiplicity which, if it is to be known, requires to be given some kind of order or structure. This ordering takes place as the result of a process of combination or synthesis, a making of unity out of diversity and multiplicity.

There are three factors involved in all our a priori knowledge: (1) the manifold of pure intuition (i.e. the spatio-temporal framework of all our experience which is provided by the nature of our capacity for receiving sense-impressions); (2) the synthesis of this manifold by means of the imagination; (3) the concepts which give unity to this synthesis. The passive side of our mental processes constitutes (1); while (2) and (3) together represent the active side—our imagination, with the help of pure concepts provided by the understanding, performs the combinatory activity which is necessary to make sense of, or give structure to, material presented to us. Just, then, as general logic provided us with a list of twelve moments or types of judgement, so transcendental logic provides us with a closely corresponding list of twelve pure concepts of the understanding (or categories).

The pure concepts of the understanding will fall exactly parallel to them [sc. the moments of the understanding in judgements in general], being nothing more than concepts of intuitions in general which are determined in themselves as judgements, necessarily and with universal validity, in respect of one or other of these moments. (*Prol.* IV 302.)

Under the heading of Quantity, we have the categories of Unity, Plurality, and Totality; under Quality, we have Reality, Negation, and Limitation; under Relation, we have (*a*) Inherence and Subsistence, (*b*) Causality and Dependence, (*c*) Community (i.e. reciprocity between agent and patient); and under Modality, (*a*) Possibility and Impossibility, (*b*) Existence and Non-existence, (*c*) Necessity and Contingency.

Kant uses the term 'category' with a direct reference to Aristotle; but he believes that his method of discovering the fundamental categories of human thought is far superior to Aristotle's, since it rests on a systematic principle, and is not simply a matter of haphazardly listing and naming all the categories one can think of. So far, however, all that Kant claims to have shown is that our minds do actually make use of these twelve categories as fundamental principles of all a priori knowledge; the question now arises, What right have we to make use of them? Given that we do have and operate with the concept of reality, for example, are we justified in assuming that the concept properly applies to anything at all? (We do after all use some concepts, such as fortune or fate, even though it might well be argued that we have no right to suppose that anything happens as a result of fortune or fate.) The categories, then, have to be provided with a deduction. The preceding section of the *Critique*, in which Kant derives his list of twelve categories from the twelve functions used in general logic, is usually called the Metaphysical Deduction, to distinguish it from the Transcendental Deduction which follows (the phrase 'Metaphysical Deduction' was used by Kant for the first time in the second edition of the *Critique*). The word 'deduction' is used in rather different senses in the two expressions. In 'Metaphysical Deduction' it means little more than systematic derivation; but in 'Transcendental Deduction' it is being used as a legal metaphor, the thought being of a lawyer deducing a title to a piece of property, for example, not of a logician or mathematician deducing conclusions from premises in a proof. The general outline of Kant's answer to the question What right have we to use the twelve categories whose existence has been established in the Metaphysical Deduction? is simple. The world as we perceive it is a world of appearances, not of things as they are in themselves (this is another way of saying that we know objects as they appear to us, not as they are in themselves). The question What right have we to suppose that the world of objects is organized according to the categories of our human understanding (that the categories can be applied to objects)? would have to be answered 'None' if it referred to things in themselves, for we cannot possibly know how they are organized. Since, however, when properly interpreted it refers to things as they appear to us, it is natural that the way things appear to us should depend in part on the structure of the minds to which they appear. This outline answer, however, needs a good deal of amplification before it can provide the deduction which Kant is looking for.

The Transcendental Deduction of the Categories was regarded by Kant as one of the most important and original parts of his entire philosophy; it is, at the same time, undoubtedly one of the most difficult, and an adequate discussion of it in a book of this size is quite impossible. I shall try to give as accurate and as clear an account of it as I can; but at best this can be no more than a general sketch of what one student of Kant takes to be the direction in which his argument is moving. The situation is further complicated by the fact that the second edition of the *Critique of Pure Reason* contains a version of the Deduction which is quite different from that which appeared in the first (though the changes, like most of the changes in the second edition, seem to be more in the method of exposition than in the actual doctrine). The account which follows is based primarily on the second edition, but occasional use is made of the first, as well as of the summary account in the *Prolegomena*.

The actual deduction in the second edition is an extremely compressed argument taking up only a few pages (B159-65); but Kant leads up to this by means of a number of explanatory and preparatory sections, some understanding of which is necessary if the final argument is to be followed.

Our empirical knowledge has two sources, sensibility and understanding. If our minds consisted of nothing but the passive ability to receive sensations, we should have a manifold or multiplicity of intuitions, but no knowledge of what this manifold contained; we should be given a variety of different shapes, colours, smells, and tastes but should not be able to name any of these things, nor even to recognize similarities and differences among them. This manifold would be spatially and temporally extended, since space and time, as was shown in the Transcendental Aesthetic, are formal conditions of all our capacity for sensing; but we should not have the concepts of space and time and should not be able to say or think that the manifold was spatially and temporally conditioned. In actual fact, of course, our situation is very different from this; we do not have to put up with so confused and unorganized a mass of sense-impressions. One of Kant's most important theses, however, is that we do not find them already organized (as we find sensations already given to us), but organize them ourselves. One of the necessary conditions of our being able to organize them is our

B

ability to recognize resemblances and differences among our sense-impressions, but this by itself is not enough. The actual organizing, and in particular the organizing of a whole audio-visual-tactile and, in general, sensuous field into a set of objects with various qualities and attributes, is the work of our intellect or understanding: the work of the spontaneous, active part of our mind, as contrasted with the receptive, passive function of sensibility. We are indeed given certain things in sensation, but it is not *given* that this object before us is a table, and that a dog; before we can know this our understanding must have formed the concepts of table and dog, and there must be some way of relating the intuition or manifold of intuition to the relevant concept—a way of bringing this particular collection of shapes, colours, etc., under the general concept of table or dog. It is worth noticing how Kant is here by implication contradicting the Cartesian belief that we are sometimes deceived, and the supposition that we may always be deceived, by our senses. People often speak of seeing with one's eyes, hearing with one's ears, and so on; and this harmless way of speaking is sometimes less harmlessly generalized by philosophers into statements about what we learn through or from our senses, and about the ways in which our senses do or may deceive us—indeed the belief that our senses may sometimes deceive us is in a way the starting-point of the entire philosophical system of Descartes. Kant wants to draw our attention, in effect, to the tendency of these philosophical statements to mislead and, in particular, he wants to stress the function of thinking, as opposed to sensing, in the origination of sense-experience.

No great philosophical difficulty arises, in Kant's view, over the formation of empirical concepts, which are formed by a comparatively simple process of abstraction; the problem concerns the formation and function of a priori concepts and especially of the fundamental a priori concepts known as the categories. What Kant sets out to show is that, just as the nature of our sensibility ensures that all that is given to it is spatially and temporally ordered, so the nature of our understanding ensures that all our knowledge, both empirical and a priori, is ordered in accordance with certain basic rules; these rules or categories are as much fundamental conditions of our thinking as space and time are fundamental conditions of our sensibility. Just as we do not discover empirically that the world is spatially ordered or that our experiences succeed one another in time, so we do not discover empirically that the world consists of substances which possess attributes, or that for everything that exists or happens there is some ground or cause of its existence or happening.

The spatio-temporal character of the world is derived from the formal character of our capacity for receiving sensations: the fact that the universe consists of substances possessing attributes and the fact that every alteration has a cause are derived from the formal character of our capacity for organizing the unorganized material provided by the senses.

We need now to look more closely at Kant's account of the organizing activity of the understanding. It takes the form essentially of an act of combination or synthesis. Whether I make an empirical judgement ('This house is higher than that tree') or an a priori one ('Every alteration has a cause'), I am judging that two or more things (using the word in its vaguest sense) are combined in reality, and this presupposes that I have myself combined them in thought.

To this act the general title 'synthesis' may be assigned, as indicating that we cannot represent to ourselves anything as combined in the object which we have not ourselves previously combined, and that of all representations *combination* is the only one which cannot be given through objects. Being an act of the self-activity of the subject, it cannot be executed save by the subject itself. (B130.)

This activity of combining itself presupposes a unity in the combining mind; any idea or representation (*Vorstellung*) must be relatable to previous and future ideas in a single consciousness.

If we were not conscious that what we think is the same as what we thought a moment before, all reproduction in the series of representations would be useless. For it would in its present state be a new representation which would not in any way belong to the act whereby it was to be gradually generated. The manifold of the representation would never, therefore, form a whole, since it would lack that unity which only consciousness can impart to it. (A103.)

This unity is called the transcendental (or synthetic) unity of apperception,[1] a 'pure unchangeable consciousness' which precedes, logically speaking, the receiving of any empirical data whatsoever. Ideas are always ideas in a single mind, which is conscious of its singleness or unity, even though it does not have to be thinking about it all the time.

[1] The term 'apperception' was introduced by Leibniz (cf. *Principles of Nature and Grace* §4: 'It is well to make distinction between the *perception*, which is the inner state of the monad representing external things, and *apperception*, which is *consciousness* or the reflective knowledge of this inner state; the latter not being given to all souls, nor at all times to the same soul.' It is through their failure to make this distinction that the Cartesians were led to what Leibniz regards as the absurd belief that animals are without souls and are mere machines: animals do have perceptions even if they are not self-consciously aware of the perceptions). Kant's use of the term is not exactly identical with that of Leibniz, but is derived from it; it means self-consciousness, together with the self-identity which is presupposed by self-consciousness.

Transcendental apperception must be distinguished from empirical apperception, or inner sense. I am empirically conscious from time to time of my mental states as they successively occur; I am conscious that I am now thinking about Kant's Transcendental Deduction of the Categories, and at this time yesterday I was conscious of the fact that I was reflecting on the possibility that it would rain within the next hour, since I wanted to go for a walk. But behind and prior to this empirical consciousness of the changing states of one's mind there lies a more fundamental principle, namely that there is a single consciousness to which all my thoughts, reflections, and intuitions are related; thoughts and intuitions do not occur in isolation but as activities of, or occurrences in, a mind which retains its numerical unity throughout the variety and difference of its activities. The mind is not, as some empiricist philosophers had suggested, simply a succession of perceptions; for if it were, no knowledge or ordered experience of any kind would be possible. On the contrary, the mind is a unity to which intuitions are given and by which they are combined. This principle of the unity of apperception is the supreme principle of all judgement and thus of all employment of the understanding.

The supreme prïnciple of the possibility of all intuition in its relation to sensibility is, according to the Transcendental Aesthetic, that all the manifold of intuition should be subject to the formal conditions of space and time. The supreme principle of the same possibility, in its relation to understanding, is that all the manifold of intuition should be subject to conditions of the original synthetic unity of apperception. In so far as the manifold representations of intuition are *given* to us, they are subject to the former of these two principles; in so far as they must allow of being *combined* in one consciousness, they are subject to the latter. For without such combination nothing can be thought or known, since the given representations would not have in common the act of the apperception 'I think', and so could not be apprehended together in one self-consciousness. (B136-7.)

This is the first important step towards the completion of the Transcendental Deduction; the next step consists of the attempt to show just how this unity of apperception determines the ways in which, and the rules according to which, our understanding works. Since the activity of the understanding consists in the making of judgements, it is clear that a further inquiry into the nature of judgement is required. We have to distinguish a judgement, which has objective reference, from a purely subjective assertion. To say 'If I support a body, I feel an impression of weight' is to say something about myself, namely that in my own perceptions the idea of body has always been connected with the idea or feeling of weight. But if I say 'Bodies are heavy', I am now expressing a judgement; for I am going beyond my own subjective ideas and asserting that the two ideas, or representations, of body and of weight are objectively combined, whatever my subjective condition may or may not be (whether, for example, I am perceiving a body, or feeling its weight, or not). Now a judgement, Kant says, as opposed to an assertion which has only subjective validity, 'is nothing but the manner in which given cognitions[1] are brought to the objective unity of apperception' (B141). In asserting that under certain conditions I feel an impression of weight I am remaining at the level of inner sense, of empirical apperception, of a purely subjective connexion between my relation to a body and my impression of weight. But in judging that bodies are heavy, I am indicating a relation in which the representations of body and weight stand to objective apperception and to its necessary unity; although 'Bodies are heavy' is an empirical, and therefore contingent, judgement,[2] nevertheless, to the extent that it is equivalent to 'I think[3] that bodies are heavy' it involves a reference to the necessary unity and identity of the thinking, judging 'I'. Now the original multiplicity of intuition does come to have a unity and is not simply a collection of unrelated impressions; and the only way in which this unity can come about is through the original synthetic unity of apperception, i.e. through the combining of intuitions into a self-identical consciousness by the activity of the understanding. But the understanding performs this activity through making a series of judgements; it follows that the combining activity must take place in accordance with the principles of judgement, i.e. in accordance with those logical functions of judgement, the table of which is provided by formal logic. And since the categories, as the Metaphysical

[1] Kant's word is *Erkenntnisse*, which Kemp Smith, here as elsewhere, translates 'modes of knowledge', an unfortunate phrase which, if it means anything at all, seems to carry a quite misleading reference to methods of acquiring knowledge. What Kant means is pieces of knowledge or (sometimes) acts of knowing; and since the English word 'knowledge' cannot be used in the plural, 'cognitions' is usually the best rendering.

[2] A judgement presupposes a judger, actual or possible; hence the judgement 'Bodies are heavy' could not be made (and thus ultimately would make no sense) if there were not one single mind or 'I' which thinks of bodies and of heaviness, and performs the act of combining the two concepts. It follows that any necessary conditions for the existence of this 'I' are necessary conditions of all judgement in general.

[3] Not of course in the idiomatic sense of 'I think that . . .' which often implies a suggestion that I may be wrong. Kant is thinking of a judgement as it is made by a judging, thinking mind; not of a judgement as an abstraction considered, as it might perhaps be considered by a logician, quite independently of any act of judging.

Deduction has shown, are these functions of judgement as they are employed in application to intuition, it follows that the manifold of any intuition is subject to the categories.

So far Kant's argument has dealt with the synthesis of a manifold of intuition in general; he now brings in a reference to the special conditions of human intuition, namely the fact that it is a sensible intuition and therefore subject to the forms of sensibility, space and time.

In the *metaphysical deduction* the *a priori* origin of the categories has been proved through their complete agreement with the general logical functions of thought; in the *transcendental deduction* we have shown their possibility as *a priori* cognitions of objects of an intuition in general. We have now to explain the possibility of knowing *a priori*, by means of *categories*, whatever objects may *present themselves to our senses*, not indeed in respect of the form of their intuition, but in respect of the laws of their combination, and so, as it were, of prescribing laws to nature, and even of making nature possible. For unless the categories discharged this function, there could be no explaining why everything that can be presented to our senses must be subject to laws which have their origin *a priori* in the understanding alone. (B159-60.)

Kant first introduces the term 'synthesis of apprehension' to stand for the combination of the manifold in an empirical intuition, whereby perception (i.e. empirical consciousness of the intuition) is possible. It is possible for me to be looking at a house without perceiving it as a house; before this perception can occur I must combine my visual impressions, and any other kinds of relevant sense-impression, into a whole or unity. (I must do this before I can recognize it as an object at all, let alone a determinate object such as a house.) Now this synthesis of apprehension must always conform to the a priori forms of sensible intuition, space and time. Space and time, however, are not merely forms of intuition, but are themselves intuitions with a manifold of their own, and the unity of this manifold is provided by the understanding (i.e. I can recognize that all the temporal and spatial phenomena of which I am cognizant belong to one time and one space). It follows, Kant thinks, that the empirical synthesis of apprehension must conform with the purely intellectual synthesis of apperception, and hence that all synthesis, where the judgements involved are empirical as well as where they are a priori, must conform to the categories. Kant gives two examples of the way in which this conformity takes place. First, when I perceive a house (as opposed to merely having a number of more or less connected sense-impressions) I think of it as necessarily extended in one space; 'I draw as it were the outline of the house in conformity with this synthetic unity of the manifold in space' (B162). This synthetic unity has its origin in the understanding; in this particular case it is the category of quantity that applies to the house, which is an extensive magnitude composed of homogeneous, measurable parts. Secondly, when I perceive the freezing of water, I apprehend two states, fluidity and solidity, standing in a temporal relation to one another. Once again there is a synthetic unity of the manifold, in this example, of time, not space; my perception presupposes a single time in which the order of events is determined (the solidity must follow the fluidity, not vice versa). Once again the unity is provided by the combinatory activity of the understanding, this time through the category of cause, which the understanding applies to everything that happens, regarding it as the effect of something preceding it in time.

The upshot of all this is that nature is subject to the categories, not because things in themselves are so subject (things in themselves have their own laws, of which we can know nothing), but because nature is nothing for us except as it appears to us, and the way in which it appears to us is determined in its general characteristics by the fact that our intellects have to apply the categories before they can make any sort of sense of the multiplicity of sense-impressions which are presented to us (and also, of course, by the fact that our capacity for receiving sense-impressions is such that we receive them in a spatial and temporal framework). This is not to say that we can discover the detailed workings of nature by intellectual reflection alone; we cannot deduce any scientific knowledge from the table of categories. Kant's point is that, although empirical investigation is necessary before scientific knowledge can be acquired, the general structure of that knowledge is something that is not discovered by empirical investigation, but is contributed by the combinatory power of the human mind. If an alteration takes place in the physical world we have to make use of observation and experiment before we can discover the cause of the alteration; but we know, without the need for observation of experiment, that it must have some cause and that this cause must be related to some event or events preceding the alteration in time.

## Analytic of Principles

The analytic of principles is a canon for judgement, instructing it how to apply the concepts of the understanding to appearances. If we regard understanding as the faculty of rules, Kant says, judgement will be the faculty of subsuming under rules, i.e. of distinguishing whether something falls under a given rule. One of the tasks of transcendental logic is to lay down rules for the employment in judgement of the pure concepts of the understanding (rules for deciding what is to count as a substance or a cause, or as unity or plurality, etc.). The most important rules are those which concern the relation of the categories to experience, and Kant discusses them in a section entitled the 'Schematism of the Pure Concepts of the Understanding'.

Whenever an object is subsumed under a concept the idea or representation of the object must be homogeneous with the concept. For example, Kant says, if we think of a plate as being circular in shape, the empirical concept of plate is homogeneous with the pure geometrical concept of a circle under which it is subsumed—the roundness which is thought in the circle is intuited in the plate. But the categories cannot be intuited, nor are they contained in appearances; how then can intuitions be subsumed under categories or pure concepts be applicable to appearances? (The Transcendental Deduction has shown that they must be applicable to appearances in some way or other, but we still do not know how.) Now since there is no homogeneity between category and appearance, and since nevertheless the appearance has in the end to be subsumed under the category, there must, Kant says, be some third thing which is homogeneous both with the category and with the appearance, and which mediates between the two; this third thing, which must clearly be in one respect intelligible and in another sensible, consists in what Kant calls the transcendental schema. The key to this is the notion of time.

The concept of understanding contains pure synthetic unity of the manifold in general. Time, as the formal condition of the manifold of inner sense, and therefore of the connection of all representations, contains an *a priori* manifold in pure intuition. Now a transcendental determination of time is so far homogeneous with the category, which constitutes its unity, in that it is universal and rests upon an *a priori* rule. But, on the other hand, it is so far homogeneous with appearance, in that time is contained in every empirical representation of the manifold. Thus an application of the category to appearances becomes possible by means of the transcendental determination of time, which, as the schema of the concepts of understanding, mediates the subsumption of the appearances under the category. (A138-9 B177-8.)

A schema is a kind of mental diagram or pattern, and its function is not limited to mediating between categories and appearances. With empirical concepts, such as the concept of dog, there is a schema produced by the imagination which has to be distinguished both from an image of a dog and from the concept of dog itself; I cannot subsume a particular concrete image under the general concept without making use of a schema which has, as it were, a foot in both worlds—it is a product of imagination, like the image, but is general, like the concept. 'The concept "dog" signifies a rule according to which my imagination can delineate the figure of a four-footed animal in a general manner, without limitation to any single determinate figure such as experience, or any possible image that I can represent *in concreto*, actually presents' (A141 B180). The situation is somewhat similar with pure sensible concepts, i.e. those of arithmetic and geometry. The concept of a triangle cannot be represented simply by an image, which will be much too particularized in form; an image of a triangle will necessarily be either right angled, acute angled, or obtuse angled, for example, but the concept of a triangle in general has to apply to all triangles, of whatever kind, and we need some general picture of the shape of a triangle which is as general as the concept but which, unlike the concept, has a direct spatial reference. Given the concept (triangle = plane three-sided figure) we can construct a schema which will show us (to put it rather crudely) what a triangle looks like, and conversely we can tell that a given figure is a triangle, without having to count the sides or refer to the definition, by simply comparing it with the schema.

But with the categories, of course, there can be no question of any corresponding image; we cannot have an image of a cause or of plurality or of substance. There is nevertheless an analogy between the relationship of empirical or mathematical concepts to their schemata on the one hand and that of the categories to theirs on the other, namely that the schemata are the necessary conditions of our being able to make use of the relevant concepts to acquire knowledge. The category becomes usable by being brought under conditions of time, and the schematized category is, in effect, a temporal version of what, in its original form, had no temporal reference. To take a simple example, the original category of substance can be defined as that which can be thought of only as subject of a judgement, and never as predicate belonging to another subject. But this, as it stands, is quite inapplicable to anything in experience, since we have no means of deciding what objects of experience can be thought of only as subjects of judgements, and thus of deciding what objects fall under the category. The schema of substance, however, is what Kant calls 'permanence of the real in time' (A143 B183); i.e. substances are those permanently existing things in and to which alterations take place in time, but which do not themselves come into being or disappear. The category of reality, again, is applicable to the objects of experience only when schematized as meaning existence in time; we cannot use the category to attain knowledge of any sort of non-temporal existence.

This need to rely on schemata is, in effect, a limitation of the understanding by sensibility (since time is the form of intuition of inner sense, in which all our thoughts, perceptions, sensations, etc., necessarily take place). The upshot is to stress once more Kant's thesis that our understanding can give us no synthetic knowledge[1] without the help of our sensibility, and that this need to rely on sensibility limits our knowledge to objects of actual or possible sense-experience. And the rest of the Transcendental Analytic produces further argument for this conclusion, and for the more far-reaching conclusion that the understanding, through its schematized categories, provides principles for the possibility of experience; it is not merely that the categories can be applied to experience, but that all our experience has to be of a kind that is in various ways limited by the fact that it is subject to the categories. I shall not attempt here to give a detailed account of this additional argument. It consists mainly of a further development of what has been said about the categories, and a more extended discussion of the ways in which they are applied to experience. Its main interest is for the manner in which it attempts to provide a foundation for a philosophy of science, and to illustrate and defend Kant's dictum that 'The order and regularity in the appearances, which we entitle *nature*, we ourselves introduce. We could never find them in appearances, had not we ourselves, or the nature of our mind, originally set them there' (A125). Kant holds that the analysis of the working of the understanding with its categories provides us with a knowledge of some fundamental necessary conditions of all human experience and knowledge; it shows us what our experience must be like, even before we can provide this experience with any empirical content. But it is important to realize that the scientist's systematic investigation of the whole of nature, as much as the ordinary man's piecemeal attempt to understand and control the small section of the physical world with which he is in contact, takes place under the limiting conditions fixed by the nature of human understanding and sensibility. The a priori principles of the understanding are, together with those of sensibility, the first principles of all human knowledge and are, at the same time, the first principles of natural science. Of course science requires data from sense-

---

[1] It can of course give us analytic knowledge, by analysis of concepts; but this is not enough to give us any mathematical, scientific, or metaphysical knowledge (we may so define 'God' . that the judgement 'God is omnipotent' is analytically true, but this does nothing to tell us whether any object corresponding to this concept of God actually exists).

experience—Kant is the last person to hold that empirical facts can be derived from pure thought without help from the senses; but the nature of the human mind prescribes, in effect, certain fundamental scientific principles. Kant's philosophy of mathematics is an offshoot, as it were, of the Transcendental Aesthetic:[1] the fundamental principles of geometry and arithmetic depend on the fact that these branches of mathematics are related, respectively, to space and time, the two forms of human sensibility. Geometry establishes synthetic a priori truths about space. For example, whatever empirical facts about space and its contents we may establish by observation, we know without the need for observation that two straight lines cannot enclose a space and that a straight line is the shortest distance between two points. Geometry determines the general properties of space, and it does so independently of any concrete, empirical evidence, deriving its conclusions from the general form which our spatial experience must take. Although arithmetic is not about time in the way in which geometry is about space, it is nevertheless, in Kant's view, as closely connected with time. The fundamental concept of arithmetic, that of numerical succession, is for human beings inevitably based on the temporal process of counting; for human beings at least, numerical succession is unintelligible except on a basis of temporal succession. We could not, Kant thinks, apprehend 6 as the numerical successor of 5 if it were not for the fact that 6 literally succeeds (comes after) 5 in the counting process. This does not mean, of course, that we have to count whenever we perform an arithmetical calculation or operate with any proposition involving numbers, and counting is impossible for very large numbers anyhow, precisely because we do not have enough time to do it; Kant's point is that the very large or complicated numbers and the sophisticated arithmetical theorems make sense, in the end, only in terms of the basic succession of the integers, and that this succession in its turn makes sense to us only because our counting is an essentially temporal process.

For analogous reasons, Kant's philosophy of science is an offshoot of the Transcendental Analytic, i.e. of the philosophical attempt to establish the concepts with which, and the principles on which, the understanding works. Each of the four groups of categories has a corresponding

---

[1] Pure mathematics, that is. The demonstration that mathematical truths apply to objects of experience (e.g. that empirical intuitions obey the a priori geometrical laws of pure intuition and that groups of discrete objects obey the laws of pure arithmetic) requires the notion of a schema; that is to say, the validity of applied mathematics is demonstrated in the Transcendental Analytic.

principle and these principles, as well as governing the activity of the understanding in general, function also as principles of natural science; they need to be supplemented, of course, before any scientific laws can be discovered, but they are presupposed by all scientific investigation.[1] The categories of quantity yield what Kant calls Axioms of Intuition, the general principle of which is that all intuitions are extensive magnitudes (in space or time as the case may be), that is, magnitudes which may be thought of as wholes made up of parts. Thus a line two feet long may be thought of as made up of four lines each six inches in length, and a period of one hour as equivalent to three periods of twenty minutes each. It is this principle that provides one ground for the application of mathematics to experience, yielding axioms in geometry (e.g. that only one straight line can be drawn between two points) and self-evident elementary propositions in arithmetic (e.g. $7 + 5 = 12$).[2] The categories of quality yield Anticipations of Perception, the principle of which is that in all appearances, the real that is the object of sensation has intensive magnitude, that is a magnitude which can be measured in degrees (not amounts, as in extensive magnitudes). Sensations of light and dark, of warmth and cold, of pleasure and pain, for example, are necessarily variable in degree, and we know this to be true independently of any knowledge gained empirically from our actual sensations. Our understanding can thus anticipate sensations and discover that they necessarily have, and therefore that what is real in the whole of appearance has, degrees. Since intensive magnitudes, like extensive ones, are in principle measurable, the anticipations of perception provide a second application of mathematics to experience.

[1] The four groups of categories also provide a framework which, when certain basic empirical concepts are brought in, can yield something intermediate between the pure (i.e. absolutely a priori) natural science of this section of the *Critique* and the empirical discoveries and generalizations that form the body of an experimental science. The concept of motion is an empirical concept (we know a priori that the objects of experience must be extended in space, but we do not know that they move in space until we observe them doing so); but in the philosophical (not scientific) work entitled *Metaphysical First Principles of Natural Science* Kant considers the whole of physics as the study of motion under four heads corresponding to the four groups of categories—(a) Phoronomy, which treats of the quantity of motion, (b) Dynamics, which treats of its quality, (c) Mechanics, which treats of the relations between motions, and (d) Phenomenology, which treats of the modality of motion.

[2] In spite of his general title 'Axioms of Intuition' Kant holds that there are no axioms, strictly speaking, in arithmetic. Such propositions as $7 + 5 = 12$, though self-evident and synthetic, are not sufficiently general to be axioms, while the basic general propositions of arithmetic such as 'If equals be added to equals the wholes are equal' are analytic, not synthetic, propositions and therefore cannot be axioms either.

The principle of the understanding which corresponds to the categories of relation (Substance, Cause, Community) yields what are called Analogies of Experience. The principle of the analogies is that experience is possible only through the representation of a necessary connexion of perceptions (as opposed to the haphazard succeeding of one perception by another), and there are three analogies which correspond to the three categories:

(i) the principle of the permanence of substance: throughout all changes in nature, the quantum of substance remains the same;

(ii) the principle of causality (or more strictly, of succession in time in accordance with the law of causality): i.e. all alterations take place in accordance with the law of cause and effect, and no alteration takes place without a cause;

(iii) the principle of coexistence: all substances, so far as they can be perceived to coexist in space, are in complete reciprocity, i.e. they all mutually interact.

Finally, the categories of modality yield Postulates of Empirical Thought; we obtain from them what are, in effect, working definitions of the three relevant categories in their application to experience. The possible is that which agrees with the formal conditions of experience, both intuitional and conceptual; the actual is that which is bound up with the material conditions of experience, i.e. sensation; and the necessary is that which in its connexion with the actual is determined in accordance with universal conditions of experience.

I shall deal with only one point in this section of the *Critique*, viz. Kant's attempt to prove the universal validity of the causal principle. Besides being of great philosophical importance in its own right, the proof is typical of Kant's approach to this type of question, and an understanding of it will make many of his other arguments easier to follow.

Hume, Kant says in the *Prolegomena* (IV 310), was right in asserting that causality is not a connexion which is demonstrable by reason—it is not a purely logical relation. But he was wrong in his belief that the only possible alternative lay in finding the concept of causality directly in experience, and that our tendency to think that some events are caused by other events preceding them in time is simply a matter of habit, for which no rational defence can be given. The principle that everything has a cause is true a priori, provided that we take care to limit its application to actual or possible experience; and this amounts to the proviso that we must interpret it as meaning that every event or alteration has a cause. Particular causal laws, again, are valid of experience, but they are valid only because of the a priori validity of the causal principle itself. It is because of this that we can pass from the assertion of a mere correlation (e.g. 'If the sun shines long enough on a body, it grows warm'), in which there is no reference to causality at all, to that of a causal law (e.g. 'The sun through its light is the cause of heat'); and Hume's treatment of causality gives an inadequate explanation of the possibility of this transition.

'The apprehension of the manifold of appearance', Kant says (A189 B234), 'is always successive.' When I observe a house, for example, my observation of it is made up of a series of successive mental acts of attention, since I am unable to observe or apprehend everything about the house at once.[1] Yet the house itself is obviously not, objectively considered, a series of successive events, in spite of the temporal succession which is necessarily involved in my subjective apprehension of it. How then can we distinguish this successive observation of a static object from the equally successive observation of what is itself objectively successive? Or in other words, how can we distinguish the apprehension of an unchanging object or condition from the apprehension of an event or alteration? Kant's answer is that in the former case the order in which the successive perceptions succeed one another is optional, according to the choice of the observer, whereas in the latter it is determined by the nature of the alteration. 'In the previous example of a house my perceptions could begin with the apprehension of the roof and end with the basement, or could begin from below and end above; and I could similarly apprehend the manifold of the empirical intuition either from right to left or from left to right' (A192 B237-8). But in the apprehension of an event, for example seeing a ship move downstream, the order of perceptions is determined by the event; I cannot first perceive the ship lower down the river and subsequently perceive it higher up. The subjective succession of apprehension, as Kant puts it, must be derived from the objective succession of appearances; and the objective succession will consist 'in that order of the manifold of appearance according to which, *in conformity with a rule*, the apprehension of that which happens follows upon the apprehension of that which precedes' (A193

[1] This is a necessary limitation of human powers of apprehension, although there may conceivably exist other beings to whom the limitation does not apply. It is not merely that we cannot *see* the whole object at once, but that we cannot *think* it all at once; our thinking is necessarily discursive and our apprehension of the house requires to be split up into sections, as it were, each section taking the form of a judgement making use of separate concepts. We have to think separately, for example, about its shape, size, and material as well as about the separate parts and sides of the house.

B238). That is to say, there is a rule which prevents the succession of apprehension being as arbitrary in direction as it could be in the case of the house, and it is only because of the existence of such rules that we can distinguish objective from subjective succession. The general form of the rule is that the event must be referred to something which precedes it and on which it follows in conformity with a rule. If there were no such antecedent event, i.e. if an event could exist without a cause preceding it in time, all succession of perception would be purely subjective, and we should never be able to assert that two states succeed one another in reality. The causal principle is thus in an important respect like space and time, clear concepts of which we can extract from experience only because we have put them into experience, i.e. only because they are formal a priori conditions of experience. So far from the causal principle being discovered through experience, experience would be impossible if the principle did not hold a priori of experience.

# 2
# The Illusions of Speculative Metaphysics

THE MOST IMPORTANT general conclusion of the Transcendental Analytic is 'that the most the understanding can achieve *a priori* is to anticipate the form of a possible experience in general' (A246 B303). It does not give us knowledge of things as they are in themselves, but only of things as they appear to us. We can use the traditional philosophical distinction between phenomena and noumena as equivalent to that between appearances and things in themselves only if we are careful not to suppose that the word 'noumena' stands for entities that can be known by the understanding (the forms or ideas of Plato, which were for him the only objects of knowledge and which were acceptable to the pure intellect—nous—alone, are the best examples of noumena in this positive sense of the word). If we are to speak of noumena we must do so, Kant insists, only in a negative sense, as meaning things in so far as they are not objects of a sensible intuition. It is illegitimate, in spite of the authority of Plato and others, to use the term in a positive sense to refer to objects of a non-sensible (i.e. intellectual) intuition, for we have no such intuition ourselves, nor can we even understand what such an intuition would be like supposing that there were any beings which possessed it.

Now any attempt to apply the categories to noumena even in the negative sense with a view to obtaining knowledge of them is bound to fail, for reasons given in the Analytic. We are not, however, prevented from using the categories to extend our thinking, as opposed to our knowledge, beyond appearances to things in themselves. We can, for example, perfectly well think (i.e. form the concept) of a substance which exists outside space and time (an eternal spiritual substance), even though Kant has shown that we can have no knowledge of such a substance— no knowledge whether it exists or of what it would be like if it did exist (except of course such knowledge as could be derived analytically from the concept itself). The failure to make this distinction between what we can know and what we can think, and the related failure to distinguish properly between appearances and things in themselves are, Kant holds, responsible for the extravagances of speculative metaphysics and for its failure to achieve the status of a science which is enjoyed by mathematics and physics. There is a kind of illusion which leads us to mistake the fundamental rules which govern our understanding for an objective determination of things as they are in themselves. It is an illusion to which we are all inevitably subject; but there is no reason why we should be deluded by it (the astronomer is as affected as anyone by the illusion that the moon is larger at its rising, but he is not in the least deluded or deceived by it). The Transcendental Analytic has explained and demonstrated the truth of the matter, namely that we are able to make true synthetic a priori judgements in mathematics and science only because it is the nature of our sensibility and understanding and the connexion between them that yield this a priori knowledge; we can make synthetic a priori judgements only about objects of possible sense-experience. The main business of the Transcendental Dialectic is to explain in detail just how the failure to distinguish appearances from things in themselves leads to errors, and particularly to the errors of speculative metaphysics.

There exists a natural and unavoidable dialectic of pure reason—not one in which a bungler might entangle himself through lack of knowledge, or one which some sophist has artificially invented to confuse thinking people, but one inseparable from human reason, and which, even after its deceptiveness has been exposed, will not cease to play tricks with reason and continually entrap it into momentary aberrations ever and again calling for correction. (A298 B354-5.)

The key to the problem of the Dialectic is the examination of the faculty of reason (*Vernunft*) in the narrow sense in which it is opposed to understanding (*Verstand*), which has been the topic of the Analytic. Reason, for Kant, is a higher faculty than understanding, just as the latter is higher than sensibility; it is a faculty of principles, whereas the understanding is a faculty of rules. The understanding, through its categories, provides rules for the systematizing and arranging of intuitions, both pure and sensible: reason, through its Ideas,[1] seeks to provide principles for the ordering of the concepts and judgements produced by the understanding. Reason undoubtedly has work to do in the field of logic; it is, according to Kant, the source of syllogistic (or mediate) inference (as opposed to immediate inference, which is the work of the understanding). Immediate inference takes place whenever we analyse the content of any subject-term in a judgement; from 'All men are mortal' we can,

---

[1] It is convenient to follow the common practice of rendering Kant's word *Idee* by 'Idea', keeping 'idea' as the equivalent of *Vorstellung*.

according to Kant, infer immediately that some mortal beings are men. But if we wish to infer from 'All men are mortal' that all learned beings are mortal we need a third, mediating judgement to bridge the gap between the two original judgements; for the concept 'learned being' does not occur in 'All men are mortal', and the desired conclusion can be reached only by the addition of the proposition that all learned beings are men.[1] Kant thinks that an examination of what happens in syllogistic inference yields an important clue about the nature and activity of the faculty of reason in general. Suppose we take a simple syllogism:

> All men are mortal (major premiss)
> All Greeks are men (minor premiss)
> ∴ All Greeks are mortal (conclusion).

'In every syllogism', Kant says (A304 B360-1), 'I first think a *rule* (the major premiss) through the *understanding*. Secondly, I *subsume* something known under the condition of the rule by means of the power of *judgement* (the minor premiss). Finally, what is thereby known I *determine* through the predicate of the rule, and so *a priori* through *reason* (the conclusion).' The important point for the elucidation of Kant's concept of reason is the notion of a condition. If we think of the syllogism as a means of proving a conclusion which we already have reason to believe may be true, we can think of the activity of reason as looking for, and finding, the condition under which the proposition which it is desired to prove is true; 'All Greeks are mortal' is true on condition that 'All men are mortal' is true. But this major premiss itself needs to be proved; i.e. we need to discover the condition of the condition, and so on. And this procedure seems unsatisfactory unless at some point or other we can expect some halt in the demand for proof; i.e. reason looks for an eventual condition which is itself unconditioned. 'The principle peculiar to reason in general, in its logical employment, is: to find for the conditioned knowledge obtained through the understanding the unconditioned whereby its unity is brought to completion' (A307 B364). If, then, reason is to have something more than a merely logical employment, there will have to be some guarantee that we can legitimately proceed from the conditioned to the unconditioned—i.e. that arguments valid of and concepts applicable to the former are valid of and applicable to the latter also (more specifically, that arguments valid of, and concepts applicable to, possible or actual experience are valid of, and applicable to, fields outside any possible experience). Kant's answer to this demand is

---

[1] *Vernunftschluss* (conclusion of reason) is Kant's ordinary word for 'syllogism'.

that, although there is a natural disposition for reason to try to achieve this transcendental purpose, speculative reason can in fact never do so; it inevitably involves itself in contradictions, the exact nature of which may vary according to context but which are in general the result of failing to distinguish properly between appearances and things in themselves. (Practical reason, as we shall see later, can provide us with a rational, moral certainty even though it cannot yield absolute logical certainty, or knowledge in the strict sense.) There are three fields in which reason seeks, vainly, to discover transcendent truth by means of its Ideas (concepts which are derived from pure concepts of the understanding, but without the limitation that they are applicable only to objects of possible sense-experience); these three fields correspond to the three different types of syllogism, categorical, hypothetical, and disjunctive. Because the condition in a categorical syllogism takes the form of a universal subject-predicate judgement (as in 'All men are mortal'), reason seeks, analogously, to discover the subject which can never be a predicate (any subject of a judgement of the understanding can become the predicate of another judgement). Because the condition in a hypothetical syllogism[1] is a hypothetical judgement (i.e. a judgement which asserts something to be true, given a certain presupposition), reason, by analogy, seeks to discover a presupposition which itself presupposes nothing further. And because the condition in a disjunctive syllogism[2] is a disjunctive judgement, reason, by analogy, seeks to discover 'such an aggregate of the members of the division of a concept as requires nothing further to complete the division' (A323 B380). The transcendental Ideas of reason thus cover three fields. There is first the field of transcendental, or rational, psychology, which is related to the categorical syllogism because the individual soul (the thinking subject, the 'I'), which is the topic of rational psychology, is the subject which can never be a predicate. Secondly, there is rational cosmology, which is related to the hypothetical syllogism because it is concerned with the sum total of all

---

[1] A hypothetical syllogism would be of the form

$$\text{If } p \text{ then } q$$
$$p, \text{ therefore } q.$$

In his *Lectures on Logic* (para. 75, IX 129) Kant points out that, since there is no middle term, this is not, strictly speaking, a syllogism at all.

[2] A disjunctive syllogism, according to Kant, would be of the form

$$p \text{ or } q \text{ or } r$$
$$\text{But not-}p \text{ and not-}r$$
$$\therefore q.$$

(The major premiss may contain any number of terms from two upwards.)

appearances (the world or universe) and with the conditions of its existence. Thirdly and finally, there is rational theology, which is connected with the disjunctive syllogism in the following way. Of any object we may say that it must possess one, and only one, of every pair of contradictory attributes. Hence in order to give a complete description of any object we would need to have a complete list of all possible attributes arranged in pairs of alternatives (the object must be A or not-A, B or not-B, and so on). From this notion of a complete list of all possible attributes we can pass to the notion of a being which possesses all possible attributes; and this being is the God of the Leibniz-Wolff-Baumgarten tradition of philosophical theology of which Kant is thinking. All these branches or aspects of speculative metaphysics involve pseudo-rational or dialectical inferences analogous to, but less secure than, the corresponding types of syllogism (mediate rational inference) which, like their dialectical counterparts, spring from the faculty of reason.[1] The three sections of the *Critique* in which the errors of metaphysics are exposed in detail are entitled, for reasons which will, I hope, become clear later, the 'Paralogisms of Pure Reason', 'The Antinomy of Pure Reason', and the 'Ideal of Pure Reason'.

## The Paralogisms of Pure Reason

A paralogism is simply a syllogism which contains a formal fallacy; but the transcendental paralogism which we meet here is an attempted syllogism in which a formally invalid conclusion is drawn from a transcendental ground. There are four such paralogisms,[2] the first seeking to prove that the soul is a substance, the second that it is simple, the third that it is a person, and the fourth that the existence of things outside one's own perceptions is doubtful. To understand the general trend of Kant's argument, we need do no more than look briefly at his treatment of the first paralogism, which he regards as the foundation of all rational psychology.

That which cannot be thought otherwise than as subject does not exist otherwise than as subject, and is therefore substance.

[1] Kant also derives these three branches of metaphysics in an apparently—though only apparently—alternative way through the three categories of relation—substance, causality, and community.

[2] In the first edition of the *Critique* Kant discusses each paralogism separately in some detail; in the second edition most of the detail is omitted and he concentrates on the general error common to all four. The change, like most of the changes in the second edition, affects the method of exposition rather than the essential doctrine, and some conflation of the two accounts is therefore legitimate.

A thinking being, considered simply as such, cannot be thought otherwise than as subject.

Therefore it exists also only as subject, that is, as substance. (B410 11.)

The argument is fallacious because the phrase 'cannot be thought otherwise than as subject' does not mean the same in the major premiss as it does in the minor. In the major premiss the thought referred to is the thought of an object in general and, therefore, of an object given in intuition (since, as the Transcendental Analytic made clear, we cannot think of objects in any other way); but in the minor premiss there is no question of any thought of an object in general, but only of thought in relation to self-consciousness. From the fact that the 'I' that thinks belongs to thought always as subject, not as predicate, it does not follow that I am a self-subsistent being or substance; to suppose that it does is, Kant thinks, to mistake purely logical considerations for metaphysical ones. The category of substance always requires an intuition before we can give it any application; we cannot, therefore, apply it to any concept of the self which is derived simply from the fact of self-consciousness, which can be given in abstraction from all concrete intuition.

In general, then, any attempt to demonstrate by theoretical argument the substantiality and permanence (i.e. immortality) of the soul must fail. Kant lays great stress, however, on the fact that, for the same reason, attempts to demonstrate the falsity of such theses must fail also; in other words it is still open to us to believe that the soul is what rational psychology claims that it is—in particular, it is open to us to argue, as Kant argues in the *Critique of Practical Reason*, that the immortality of the soul is a postulate of practical reason and a presupposition of morality.

## The Antinomy of Pure Reason

The situation which exists as a result of metaphysical attempts to establish transcendent truths in cosmology differs in one important respect from that which arises from attempts to establish similar truths about the soul. As far as rational psychology is concerned, the error and illusion are in one direction only: we appear (misleadingly) to be able to prove that the soul is a simple permanent substance and that the existence of external objects is doubtful, but there is not even a suggestion of any metaphysical argument which, however fallacious, might seem to prove the contrary. In cosmology, however, we have an antinomy —i.e. we find arguments which are apparently of equal validity used to prove two contradictory conclusions. We have in fact, as has already been

stated, four antinomies, each containing a thesis and an antithesis together
with a seemingly valid proof:

1. *Thesis*: The world has a beginning in time and is limited as regards space.
   *Antithesis*: The world is infinite in both time and space.
2. *Thesis*: Every composite substance in the world is made up of simple
   parts, and nothing anywhere exists save the simple or what is composed
   of the simple.
   *Antithesis*: No composite thing in the world is made up of simple
   parts, and there nowhere exists anything simple.
3. *Thesis*: Causality in accordance with laws of nature is not the only
   causality from which the appearances of the world can one and all be
   derived. To explain these appearances it is necessary to assume that there
   is also a causality of freedom.
   *Antithesis*: There is no freedom; everything in the world takes place
   solely in accordance with laws of nature.
4. *Thesis*: There belongs to the world, either as its part or as its cause,
   a being that is absolutely necessary.
   *Antithesis*: An absolutely necessary being does not exist in the world,
   nor does it exist outside the world as its cause.

The four theses belong to what Kant calls a dogmatic approach: the
antitheses are the arguments of empiricism. From a practical point of
view, it would be advantageous to be able to prove the theses—in particular, the thesis of the third antinomy seems to be required by morality;
and philosophically speaking, the acceptance of the theses would allow us
to arrange our knowledge in a thoroughly systematic way, beginning
with an unconditioned condition as a fundamental underivative principle,
and proceeding to the subordinate factors regarded as consequences.
Empiricism, on the other hand, seems to make morality impossible,
and can never reach a first principle which would provide the basis of a
philosophical system; it has, on the other hand, the great advantage of
limiting its claims to possess knowledge to the field of experience. The
solution of the problem will not consist in a demonstration that one side
to the dispute is completely right and the other completely wrong.
Rather, a critical solution, in Kant's special sense of the word 'critical',
will show, both that the dogmatist's claim to possess knowledge of the
truth of the four theses must be firmly rejected, and that, in spite of this,
the empiricist is mistaken if, espousing a perverse dogmatism of his own,
he supposes that he has successfully refuted all possibility of believing
the theses to be true. Within the world of sense-experience, what the

empiricist says is correct; but we can think about, and have beliefs about, matters that transcend experience, provided that we do not make the dogmatist's mistake of supposing that we can have knowledge of them. The fault of both parties, in Kant's view, is that they have not understood the distinction between appearances and things in themselves; once this is grasped, the antinomies can be resolved.

As far as the first antinomy is concerned, to argue that the world, considered as a thing in itself, is finite in space or time (or, conversely, that it is infinite) is, Kant thinks, an activity that can achieve no success; for it presupposes a notion of the world as an absolute, complete totality, which is something we can never apprehend as long as we remain within the field of possible experience. We can never learn from experience that we have examined all possible appearances; the series of appearances is indefinite both spatially and temporally. The doctrine that the world is finite and the doctrine that it is infinite both require us to do something that is in principle impossible, viz. to infer theoretically a conclusion about things in themselves from propositions which refer only to appearances. What we may legitimately do, in Kant's view, is to make use of a principle of reason regulatively, as opposed to constitutively; that is, we may apply it as a rule for the consideration of appearances. The relevant rule for the first antinomy is that, however far we may have proceeded in our search for empirical conditions, we should never assume that we have reached a limit, but should always endeavour to advance further, to the next empirical condition; we must assume that the world, as appearance, is indefinitely extended in space and time— what the world is, considered as a thing in itself or noumenon, we cannot possibly know, nor can theoretical investigation by itself give us any ground for belief.

An exactly similar solution is provided for the second antinomy: whether the world, as noumenon, is made up of simple substances is a question which is unanswerable by speculative reason, which can only give us the rule that, in our empirical investigations, we should never assume that we have reached a simple and incomposite object, but should always pursue our inquiries on the assumption that the series is indefinite.

The third and fourth antinomies, however, present somewhat different problems. The first two were such that both thesis and antithesis, as applied to appearances, were false. Thesis and antithesis were logical contraries, not contradictories, and the truth lay in a third possibility, the operative concept being neither the finite nor the infinite, but the indefinite. With the third and fourth antinomies, what Kant calls dynamical, as opposed to mathematical, concepts are involved; that is, we are no longer concerned simply with the extension or the division of magnitudes, where it is essential to remain within the limits of experience, and to preserve a homogeneous approach. In dealing both with the principle of causality and with the connexion between what is contingent and what is necessary we are entitled to bring into consideration a possible connexion between the world of appearance and a purely intelligible condition (something heterogeneous), and this leads to the conclusion that, when properly interpreted, the thesis and the antithesis of the third and fourth antinomies are not both false, but both true.

We can conceive of two, and only two, kinds of causality. Causality according to nature consists in the connexion between one state and a preceding state on which it follows in accordance with a rule; causation of this kind takes place in time, and every such cause must have a cause of the same kind—it is a causality of happenings or events. Causality according to freedom is the power of beginning a state spontaneously, not under the influence of a previously occurring cause. Kant has already shown that all appearances are connected by natural causality; the question he now faces is whether spontaneous causality is thus altogether excluded. 'Is it a truly disjunctive proposition to say that every effect in the world must arise *either* from nature *or* from freedom; or must we not rather say that in one and the same event, in different relations, both can be found?' (A536 B564). There is no question of finding events in the world of appearance which are exempt from the law of natural causality; the question is only whether any place can be found for the other type of causality as well. If appearances were things in themselves, there could be no freedom at all; we can consider an event as the effect of freedom only by regarding it in a different light (from a different point of view) from that in which we regard it (inevitably) as the effect of natural necessity. So if causality through freedom is possible, we must be able to say that from one point of view (considered as phenomenon) the event is determined by natural causality, whereas from another (considered as noumenon) it is determined by freedom. Now we do not know whether any effects are in fact produced by a causality based on freedom, and even in the *Critique of Practical Reason* Kant will do no more than attempt to show that practical reason requires us to postulate that causality through freedom is possible, and in particular that men can act in contradiction to all empirical determination through the sensibility (that is, contrary to all feelings, appetites, and sensuous desires) if their duty (the moral law) requires them to. Here, in the

*Critique of Pure Reason,* Kant wants to show merely that there is no contradiction between the two kinds of causality; men's actions have both an empirical and an intelligible character, and they are naturally determined in respect of the former but capable, in theory at least, of being spontaneously produced in respect of the latter. A man's behaviour can be causally explained by reference to various factors preceding it in time—his upbringing, environment, ancestry, state of health, etc.; one can give physiological or psychological explanations of the conduct of an individual or, if one is an anthropologist, of human conduct in general. All this, however, remains at the empirical level, the level of what is observable. But we can consider human behaviour in quite another way, or from quite another point of view; for whatever a man may have done in fact, it is quite possible that he ought to have done something quite different. This concept of 'ought' is derived from reason; it is reason, in its practical, not its speculative form, that prescribes the law or rule according to which we ought to conduct ourselves, and sometimes, perhaps, men do obey this law of reason even though it leads them to act contrary to their own inclinations. If this happens, i.e. if reason ever exercises causality, man's action in its intelligible character is free, even though in its empirical character it remains subject to ordinary causal laws. But reason itself is not subject to the form of time (which conditions only sensibility); hence reason can begin a causal series without this beginning itself being conditioned or determined by something preceding it in time. Kant illustrates this point by one of his rare examples, that of a malicious lie which has been the cause of some 'confusion in society'. The investigation into the causes of the agent's telling the lie is, Kant insists, quite irrelevant to the question whether he can properly be blamed or held responsible for it. We may be able to attribute the action to such sources as bad education, or bad company, or to various aspects of the man's natural disposition (e.g. levity or thoughtlessness); but however sure we may be that the action, in its empirical character, is entirely determined by such factors, this in no way prevents us from holding the agent to blame. 'Our blame', Kant says (A555 B583),

is based on a law of reason whereby we regard reason as a cause that irrespective of all the above-mentioned empirical conditions could have determined, and ought to have determined, the agent to act otherwise. . . . Reason, irrespective of all the empirical conditions of the act, is completely free, and the lie is entirely due to its default.

Kant's treatment of the fourth antinomy is in one respect analogous to that of the third: once again the suggestion is that the thesis and the antithesis may both be true, provided that the words in them which indicate an apparent contradiction are differently interpreted. If appearances were things in themselves, there could be no necessary unconditioned being to serve as the condition of all other existence, for the world of appearance contains only contingent, not necessary, being. But although everything in the world of sense is contingent and its existence is therefore empirically conditioned, it is conceivable that there may exist a non-empirical condition of the whole series of empirically conditioned, contingent beings; that is, that there might exist a necessary being outside (as it were) the world of appearance, which would be the intelligible condition of the entire world of appearance. Thus we must not look, as the dogmatic philosophers have done, for a supernatural being to explain the existence of any particular empirical beings; the existence of any of these last is dependent solely on empirical conditions and needs no further explanation. What we can do, however, is suppose that the sensible world as a whole depends for its existence on the existence of some non-sensible, i.e. intelligible, being.[1] Once again, Kant is not arguing for the existence of such a being; he is merely arguing against the view that its existence is impossible.

## The Ideal of Pure Reason

An ideal of reason in general, according to Kant, is an individual being thought of as possessing all the qualities essential to beings of that type; the ideal of humanity is conceived as a perfect human being, a kind of archetype by reference to which the copy can be completely determined (that is, by reference to which we can measure ourselves and our imperfections against the ideal standard prescribed by reason). The transcendental ideal, the ideal of pure reason, is the concept of the *ens realissimum*, the most perfect and complete being, possessing all possible attributes (this way of regarding God is not an invention of Kant's, but forms the central notion of much philosophical theology, especially that of a Leibnizian or Wolffian kind). Now just as we can make use of the ideal of humanity without presupposing the actual existence of a perfect man, so we can make use of the concept of the perfect, highest being, without assuming the existence of anything corresponding to the concept. We can recognize our own moral imperfections without having to assume that there has ever been a morally perfect man; we can recognize

---

[1] The German word *Wesen*, which can hardly be translated in any other way, does not have the personal implications of the English word 'being'. It means any existing thing or person, whether animate or inanimate.

the relatively imperfect (from a metaphysical point of view) reality of everything that exists in the world without having to assume the existence of an absolutely perfect being. However, the attempt to prove the existence of the perfect being is inherent in human reason, and Kant therefore thinks it necessary to show just what is wrong with such attempted proofs (once again, it is the attempted proof by means of speculative reason that is objected to; the rational defence of belief in God's existence as a postulate of practical reason is another matter). All possible attempts to prove the existence of God by means of speculative reason fall, according to Kant, into one of three classes, (i) ontological, (ii) cosmological, and (iii) physico-theological; the first abstracts from all experience, the second argues from experience of existence in general, and the third argues from the specific nature of existence as it actually is.

## (i) *The ontological proof*

By 'ontological proof' Kant means the attempt[1] to prove the existence of God by a direct argument from the concept of God. God, by definition, is the *ens realissimum*, the being that possesses all reality, the absolutely perfect being; but a being which possessed all the attributes of perfection, excluding that of existence, would be less perfect than one which possessed all those attributes, including that of existence. It follows that the absolutely perfect being must possess the attribute of existence, i.e. God necessarily exists. It is as much a contradiction to claim that God does not exist as it is to claim that there can be a triangle which does not have three angles.

Kant's first objection to this is that the analogy with the triangle is a misleading one. If we have a triangle before us, then it must admittedly have three angles; we should contradict ourselves if we said that there existed a triangle with more, or fewer, than three angles. But there is no contradiction in saying that the figure before us is not a triangle, nor indeed in saying that there are no such figures as triangles; the latter proposition is obviously untrue, but it is not self-contradictory. The proper analogy would be with a proposition such as 'God is omnipotent'; to deny this would indeed be a contradiction, for omnipotence is included in the concept of God as an infinite being. The contradiction, however, consists in asserting that there is an infinite being and at the same time denying that he is omnipotent; there is no contradiction in rejecting the existence of an infinite being altogether. In general terms, that is, given

---

[1] Kant has principally in mind the form of the argument which is found in Descartes' *Meditations*; the argument itself is, however, much older than Descartes.

a subject-concept, there are certain predicates which attach analytically to that concept in such a way that we cannot reject them without contradiction; but this does not mean that we cannot reject the subject and the analytically attached predicates together.

The supporters of the ontological proof, however, while not necessarily dissenting from this general argument, often claim that the concept of the infinite being, the *ens realissimum*, is a special case, which is not subject to this objection. The infinite being by definition, it is argued, possesses all reality (in this being unlike triangles or any other members of the class of possibly existing things), and all reality must include existence; it follows that we still cannot deny the existence of the infinite being without contradiction. Kant's retort to this is more far-reaching: it is the attempted ontological proof that commits the contradiction in introducing the concept of existence into the concept of the thing (here the perfect being) which is under consideration. The proposition that this or that thing exists is either analytic or synthetic. If the proposition 'the perfect being exists' is analytic then it is indeed self-contradictory to deny it, but this is only because the proposition itself, so interpreted, is what Kant calls a 'miserable tautology' (A597 B625); it means no more than that the perfect being is a being. But if there is a perfect being, it is of course tautologous to say that it is a being, and even if there is not, it is still tautologous to say that if there were a perfect being, it would be a being—no conclusion about its actual existence can be drawn in this way. On the other hand, if the proposition 'the perfect being exists' is synthetic (as Kant indeed believes all existential propositions must be), then to deny the existence of this, or any other, being cannot involve a contradiction; for it is an essential feature of synthetic, as opposed to analytic judgements, that they can be denied without contradiction.

The main reason, in Kant's view, for the stubbornness of the belief in some form of ontological proof lies in a failure to see that 'being' or 'existence' is not a real predicate at all. It is admittedly a logical predicate, but this means no more than that we can legitimately assert that this or that thing exists: it is not a real or determining predicate, i.e. it is not a predicate which can be added to the concept of a thing.

By whatever and by however many predicates we may think a thing—even if we completely determine it—we do not make the least addition to the thing when we further declare that this thing *is*. Otherwise, it would not be exactly the same thing that exists, but something more than we had thought in the concept; and we could not, therefore, say that the exact object of my concept exists. (A600 B628.)

In other words, the thought or concept of a thing is not affected by any consideration of whether a thing corresponding to that concept exists. The thought of 100 real thalers is no different, qua thought, from the thought of 100 non-existent ones; it is not the thought or concept, but the actual state of affairs, that differs according as they exist or not. Similarly, my concept or thought of God is quite independent of the question whether a being corresponding to that concept exists; the atheist is denying the very same proposition that the theist asserts. In the case of the thalers, or of any objects the assertion of whose existence is empirical, there does not even appear to be a problem; to say that an object of possible experience actually exists is merely to say something about the object's relation to actual, as opposed to merely possible, experience, and there is no possibility of confusing the concept of such an object with its existence. But the existence of God, as it is asserted by the ontological argument, has nothing to do with experience, actual or possible; it is not asserted that God, the perfect being, could ever be met with in experience. Hence we have no means whatsoever of knowing that God exists, because in general we can never have knowledge of anything outside the limits of possible sense-experience. This is not to say that the concept of a supreme being is not a useful idea (its usefulness will be especially demonstrated in the *Critique of Practical Reason*); but it is an idea which, whatever its usefulness may be, cannot provide us with any knowledge.

## (ii) *The cosmological proof*

This argues from contingent to necessary existence. If anything exists, an absolutely necessary being must exist, as the ultimate cause of that thing's existence. But something does exist, for I at least exist; therefore, an absolutely necessary being exists. But this absolutely necessary being must be the supreme being, the *ens realissimum* of rational theology.

The necessary being can be determined in one way only, that is, by one out of each possible pair of opposed predicates. It must therefore be *completely* determined through its own concept. Now there is only one possible concept which determines a thing completely *a priori*, namely, the concept of the *ens realissimum*. The concept of the *ens realissimum* is therefore the only concept through which a necessary being can be thought. (A605 B633.)

The necessary being must be the supreme, perfect being, i.e. God.

Kant thinks this argument is riddled with fallacies; and the latter part of it is, he maintains, open to the objections already brought against the ontological argument, because it assumes that from the concept of the

highest reality it is possible to infer the existence of something corresponding to that concept. But the earlier section of the argument is also
objectionable, though for different reasons. The main objection to it is
that it passes, illegitimately, from a concept of causation which is
applicable only within the sensible world to that of a causation whereby
something outside the sensible world has an effect on something in that
world. Descartes had argued that his existence must have a cause and that
in determining this cause, although one might refer to his parents, and to
their parents, and so on, it was impossible to produce any satisfactory
final explanation of his existence without going beyond the limits of
ordinary empirical causation and attributing it to God as ultimate cause.
But the principle of causality, Kant has shown, is applicable only in the
sensible world and has no meaning outside it; hence to attribute the
existence of any contingent being or thing to the efficacy of God as its
ultimate cause is not only not a finally satisfactory explanation, it is no
explanation at all, for we can have no knowledge of the existence of such
a being and no knowledge of the way in which its causality would be
exerted if it did exist.

The notion of the supreme being, Kant concludes, is an ideal of reason,
but it must be regarded as a principle which is to regulate our thinking,
not as one by which any objective existence can be constituted. The
principle 'directs us to look upon all connection in the world *as if* it
originated from an all-sufficient necessary cause' (A619 B647); but
whether it does so originate or not is a question on which speculative
reason is unable to make any objective pronouncement.

(iii) As to *the physico-theological proof* of God's existence (this is Kant's
name for what is usually known as the argument from design) this,
although it is perhaps the most natural and, in Kant's strongly expressed
view, psychologically the most effective of all arguments for the existence
of God, is in the end no more successful than the others, considered as
an attempt at strict proof, however valuable it may be for strengthening
religious belief and for fostering our study and extending our knowledge
of nature. We find in the universe signs of an order and purposiveness
that could not have come about by mere chance or by the operation of
inanimate causes alone; by analogy with our knowledge of human wisdom
and design, we conclude that there must be a wise cause of this design
in the universe working through intelligence. But apart from the general
difficulty which is involved in arguing from empirical facts to a non-
empirical conclusion, such arguments, Kant thinks, are not sufficient to

prove what they set out to prove. It might be conceded for the sake of argument that they give grounds for believing in a divine architect, but they give none for believing in a divine creator; it might be conceded for the sake of argument that they give grounds for believing in a divine being of great wisdom and great power, but they give none for believing in an all-wise and omnipotent deity. Yet this is what the proof, at least when it is used by Christians, sets out to do; and in order to meet this objection, all it can do is surreptitiously make use of the cosmological argument as a kind of bridge between the empirical generality that it starts from and the intelligible totality it is supposed to reach—and this argument has already been refuted.

Kant concludes this section of the *Critique* by stressing that his refutation of attempts to prove the existence of God by the use of speculative reason carries with it a corresponding refutation of any attempts that might be made to disprove it or to argue that, although there may exist a divine being (or beings), its wisdom, knowledge, and power are less than infinite. We can draw no conclusions at all about the existence or attributes of God from speculation.

Thus, while for the merely speculative employment of reason the supreme being remains a mere *ideal*, it is yet *an ideal without a flaw*, a concept which completes and crowns the whole of human knowledge. Its objective reality cannot indeed be proved, but also cannot be disproved, by merely speculative reason. (A641 B669.)

Moral theology, as we shall see, can make good the deficiency; although it cannot give us knowledge, in the strict sense, of the existence and attributes of God, it can provide, from the side of practical reason, grounds for belief.

Before we proceed to consider Kant's moral philosophy, it may be as well to summarize the position so far reached. Kant believes himself to have justified the assumption with which the *Critique* began—that an examination of the structure and operation of the human intellect would provide a solution to the problem created by the existence of conflicts within metaphysics. He believes that in the course of solving this problem he has established certain fundamental truths about the principles and scope of mathematics and the physical sciences, as well as of ordinary sense-experience, and that he has thereby explained both how knowledge can be obtained in these fields and why it is impossible in the field of speculative metaphysics. There are thus two stages in the argument: first, the human mind necessarily has a certain clearly defined structure and works according to certain clearly defined laws; secondly, because of this, mathematics and physics are sciences through which men can acquire systematic knowledge, whereas metaphysics as traditionally practised is not. The great objection to traditional speculative metaphysics is that it claims to demonstrate truths in matters that go completely outside the bounds of possible sense-experience; but Kant has proved, he thinks, that the knowledge which the human mind can attain is limited by the very nature of that mind to knowledge of appearances, as opposed to things in themselves. This general conclusion from a philosophical description of the structure of the human mind to the impossibility of speculative metaphysics has affinities with the comparable procedure of Hume; what distinguishes Kant's position from Hume's is partly its far higher degree of system and generality and partly its a priori, as opposed to empirical, status. For Hume, there can be no idea that does not spring from a preceding impression: all knowledge is empirical except that which refers to what he calls 'relations between ideas', i.e. to logical or conceptual truths. For Kant, as we have seen, synthetic a priori judgements are of central importance; a great deal of our knowledge is neither limited to the logical or conceptual kind (to the sphere of what Kant calls analytic judgements) nor derived from sense-experience.

It is impossible in a work of this scope to provide any adequate assessment of this position of Kant's; but it may be worth while to mention briefly some of the points which have been most strongly criticized or queried by later philosophers. The first concerns the status of Kant's main theses in the philosophy of mind. How does Kant *know*, it may be asked, that our mental activity is the result of a combination or co-operation of sensibility and understanding, and that each of these has the structure and content which he assigns to it? There are, of course, some attempts at proof as far as the more specific descriptions are concerned, even though not all of these attempts succeed;[1] but on the fundamental issues a good deal seems to be taken for granted. This happens, no doubt, because even someone as determined as Kant is to achieve systematic completeness for his philosophy will sometimes decide that it is unnecessary to try to prove a thesis on which all his contemporaries

---

[1] An obvious failure seems to be the Metaphysical Deduction. Given that there are just these twelve functions or classifications of judgement, it is perhaps reasonable to conclude that there must be just twelve pure concepts of the understanding corresponding to these functions; the premiss itself, however, is apparently not thought by Kant to require justification, but is assumed to be an indubitable truth of logic.

and immediate predecessors would agree; the discontent is felt by philosophers of a later generation who are not only interested in the controversies between Kant and his opponents but also find doubts and difficulties in some of the views which they agreed in accepting.

A second point of difficulty concerns the conclusions which Kant draws about the nature of mathematics and physics. His arguments for the synthetic a priori nature of mathematical judgements have met with much opposition, and his attempt to establish a necessary connexion between arithmetic and the notion of time has been widely held to be unsuccessful. As for physics, it seems clear that Kant's account of its philosophical principles is more suited to the Newtonian physics of his own day than to the science as it has since developed—a fact which is hardly surprising, but which is awkward for a philosopher who claims to be enunciating permanent a priori truths about experience, not merely empirical, and thus perhaps transitory, ones.

Thirdly and finally, there is the distinction between appearances and things in themselves, which has perhaps proved the major stumbling-block to an acceptance of the major theses of Kant's philosophy. The part played by the distinction is so fundamental to Kant's whole philosophy that if it could be shown to be incoherent or otherwise unjustified, the entire system of the three *Critiques* would need to be drastically revised, if not completely rewritten. Most attacks on it take one of two forms. Some realist philosophers argue that Kant's view implies the absurd proposition that knowledge can make a difference to what is known; whereas it is obvious from the nature of knowledge—or from the meaning of the verb 'to know'—that if a man knows something to be in a certain condition, it must be in that condition quite independently of his knowing it. It follows that the perceptual knowledge which we derive through our sense-impressions must be knowledge of the perceived objects as they really are, for otherwise it would not be knowledge at all. Other critics, regarding the matter from a more idealist point of view, have argued that the only proper contrast with an object as it appears under certain conditions is with that same object, not as it supposedly is in itself independently of the way it appears, but as it appears under a different set of conditions. I may, it is said, contrast the table as it appears to me with the table as it appears, say, to a cat or an angel or God; but the notion of the table as it really is, in abstraction from all appearance, is completely meaningless.

C

# 3
# Practical Philosophy

MORALITY FOR KANT is reason in action; hence the critical examination of practical reason is at the same time a search for the supreme principle of morality. Just as the Transcendental Aesthetic of the first *Critique* is fundamental to the philosophy of mathematics, and the Transcendental Analytic to the philosophy of science, so the *Critique of Practical Reason* is fundamental to moral philosophy. In much the same way, also, it confines itself for the most part to fundamental questions; one should not look to it for a complete exposition of Kant's moral philosophy as a whole, and indeed there is no single work in which such an exposition can be found. The four major works of the critical period which have to be taken into account are, in order of publication:

(i) *Grundlegung zur Metaphysik der Sitten* (Groundwork, or Fundamental Principles, of—or, more strictly, for—the Metaphysic of Morals). This work, which is usually referred to simply as the *Grundlegung*, was published in 1785. It is in effect a preliminary section for a Critique of Practical Reason, directed to the discovery of the supreme principle of morality, but approaching this problem from what Kant calls 'ordinary rational knowledge' about morality, and making no attempt to show how this knowledge stems from the nature of reason itself.

(ii) The *Critique of Practical Reason*, published in 1788. This is a full-scale examination of the practical activity of reason and of the presuppositions involved in that activity. Taken together with the *Grundlegung*, it represents the most abstract side of Kant's ethics, concentrating as it does on the moral conduct required of man as a rational being without bringing in, except in an incidental way, considerations derived from his specific nature as a human being.

(iii) *Religion within the Bounds of Reason Alone*, published in 1793 (Part I separately in 1792). The relevant sections of this contain an account of the evil principle in man and a discussion of the relations between morality, religion, and theology.

(iv) The *Metaphysik der Sitten* (Metaphysic of Morals), published in 1797. This is a systematic working-out in their application to human beings of the rational principles of morality laid down in the *Grundlegung* and the *Critique of Practical Reason.*

The main theses of the first *Critique* could be fully understood without investigating their application to mathematics and the physical sciences in any detail; Kant's *Metaphysische Anfangsgründe der Naturwissenschaft* (Metaphysical First Principles of Natural Science) supplements the *Critique* but adds little to our understanding of it. With Kant's moral philosophy, however, the situation is different. Important though it may be to exclude all consideration of human nature and of the eventual application of the moral law from one's investigation into the supreme principle of morality (and Kant repeatedly insists on the importance of this), to confine one's attention to this abstract investigation can give only a distorted view of his moral philosophy as a whole. In this chapter, therefore, although I shall begin by expounding the main theses of the second *Critique* (making occasional supplementary use of the *Grundlegung*), I shall go on to consider the way in which Kant connects his critical investigation with the more concrete application of the principles discovered by it.

Kant's major problem in the *Critique of Practical Reason* is to show that, and how, pure reason by itself can determine the will. If this were not possible, he thinks, the whole of morality would be an illusion; action on impulse or in accordance with desire or inclination is, like everything else that is empirically grounded, subject to the laws of physical causality, and all talk of 'ought' is therefore here irrelevant—an 'ought' can arise only when man has a choice between doing what his inclinations, if unchecked by reason, would inevitably lead him to do, and doing what reason tells him is in accordance with the moral law. Moral laws are laws of freedom, as opposed to laws of nature; and man's conduct must somehow come under the first kind of law if there is to be such a thing as morality.

Apart from a few pages at the end of the *Critique of Practical Reason* on the best method of educating people in correct moral standards, the work is divided simply into an Analytic and a Dialectic, the principle of division being analogous to that observed by the first *Critique*. The Analytic demonstrates the true principles of morality: the Dialectic examines the errors into which the judgements of practical reason tend to fall and, arising out of this examination, establishes the immortality of the soul and the existence of God as postulates of pure practical reason—i.e. as truths which are presupposed by morality even though, as was argued in the first *Critique*, they cannot be theoretically proved.

A practical principle may be either subjective or objective. It is subjective when the agent regards it as applying only to himself (e.g. 'Whenever I see any chance of increasing my wealth without risk, I will take it'): objective when it is regarded as valid for all men or, more strictly, for all rational beings (e.g. 'Whenever one sees a human being in distress, one ought to help him'). Subjective principles are called maxims: objective principles are laws. Perfectly rational beings, if there are any, invariably determine their wills according to objective laws; that is, they invariably will in accordance with rational moral principles. Animals and, indeed, all things in nature except man, behave in accordance with laws of nature, not in accordance with principles (cf. *Grundlegung* IV 412, 'Everything in nature works in accordance with laws. Only a rational being has the power to act *in accordance with his idea* of laws—that is, in accordance with principles—and only so has he a *will*'). Man, as a partially or imperfectly rational being, is in a unique position; he can act in accordance with rational principles but does not invariably do so. To man alone, therefore, the notions of 'ought' and 'duty' apply, and only men can be affected by what Kant calls 'imperatives'. Imperatives (which are formulas in which practical principles of reason are expressed) are of two kinds, hypothetical or conditional, and categorical or unconditional. If the action commanded or prescribed in the imperative is good or necessary only as a means to the attainment of something else, the imperative is hypothetical: if the action commanded or prescribed is good in itself or absolutely necessary, it is categorical. 'If you want to have a prosperous old age, you must work hard in your youth' is a hypothetical imperative—one can always avoid the prescription by giving up the end. But 'You ought never to tell lies' is a categorical imperative: there is no way of evading the command or the moral requirement of practical reason which it expresses, for no end is mentioned and there is therefore no end which can be given up. Categorical imperatives and the practical laws which they embody refer only to the will itself, not to anything that may be achieved by the causality of the will. Morality, Kant is saying, cannot be regarded as a set of rules which prescribe the means necessary to the achievement of a given end, whether the end be the general happiness, or human perfection, or self-realization, or anything else; its rules must be obeyed without consideration of the consequences that will follow from doing so or not doing so. A practical principle which presupposes a desired object as the determining ground of the will cannot give rise to a practical, moral law, but can only remain at an empirical level; that is, the morality of an act of will cannot be determined by the matter or content of the will, for when the will is materially, i.e. empirically, determined, the question of its morality does not arise. Kant is not saying here, as some commentators have supposed, that some human actions or volitions have no object, end, or purpose—on the contrary, he explicitly states that all actions or volitions have an object; what he is saying is that the morality of an action or volition is not determined by the object which is achieved by it, or which the agent intends to achieve.

This consideration leads Kant to one of his most important and characteristic theses. If the moral character of willing is not determined by the matter or content of what is willed, it must be determined by the form: 'If a rational being can think of its maxims as practical universal laws, he can do so only by considering them as principles which contain the determining grounds of the will because of their form and not because of their matter' (KPV v 26-27). But if we abstract from all material content of the will, that is from all thought of an objective or purpose that is to be achieved by action, we are left, Kant says, with nothing but the merely formal property of the universality of the rule or law that governs the will; in other words, the morality of a maxim is determined by its suitability for functioning as a universal law, applicable not just to the willing of this particular agent here and now, but to that of any agent in a situation of the same general type. An important consequence follows from this connexion of morality with the concept of a universal law. Since a moral will must be so in virtue of its form alone, the will must be capable of a purely formal determination; that is, it must be possible for a man to act (or, more strictly, to will) in a certain way for the sole reason that willing in this way is prescribed by a universal law, no matter what empirical results may be achieved by willing in this or any other way. And this amounts to saying that a will to which moral considerations apply must be, in the strictest sense, a free will, one that can function, even though it does not always function, independently of the laws of natural causality. In other words, we are first presented with the concept of morality; this has to be explained in terms of a universal moral law, and the ability to will in obedience to such a law leads us to postulate the freedom which, as we have seen, could not be demonstrated by speculative metaphysics. The freedom that has been established, however, is not a merely negative freedom consisting in the absence of constraint by empirical causes; it is a positive freedom which consists in the ability to make acts of will in accordance with the moral law for no other reason than that they are in accordance with it (or as Kant often puts it, out of respect, or reverence, for the law). Freedom in this positive sense is called the autonomy of the will, and its absence (i.e. any situation in which the will is determined by external sources) is called heteronomy. The point is that in obeying the moral law for the sake of the law alone, the will is autonomous because it is obeying a law which it imposes on itself: heteronomy occurs whenever the will obeys laws, rules, or injunctions from any other source.

It is important to realize that in what he says about autonomy and universality Kant does not regard himself as making a philosophical discovery of a moral criterion or principle which the ordinary non-philosophical man does not understand and which he has to accept on the philosopher's authority; there is no question, as there is with Plato for instance, of philosophy being able to discover important moral truths inaccessible to the non-philosophical mind. All that Kant claims to be doing at this point is to state a moral principle which is in fact employed by ordinary people in their moral deliberation and thinking (even though he may state it more precisely and technically than they do) and to explain how the validity of the principle follows from philosophical considerations about the nature of reason and of the contrast between causal necessity and freedom.

Kant attempts to demonstrate in a systematic way that all previous efforts to provide a fundamental principle of morality have offended against the requirement that such a principle must refer only to the form of the will, not to its matter. Many suggested principles have been empirical, and therefore obviously inadequate; the principle that morality consists in doing whatever will contribute most to the agent's physical pleasure, for example (a view which Kant somewhat misleadingly attributes to Epicurus), or that one's whole duty consists in obeying the laws of the political society of which one is a member. There are also, however, some a priori principles which, no matter how important obedience to them may be, cannot function as fundamental principles of morality; these are the principle of perfection (which Kant attributes to the Leibnizian Wolff and the Stoics) and the principle that one's duty consists in doing the will of God. We cannot regard a man's perfection (in the sense of his fitness for any kind of end or purpose, i.e. his talent or skill) as the ultimate moral principle, for the moral value of perfection will clearly depend on the morality of the ends which it is to serve. And although Kant thinks that morality can in a sense be regarded as consisting in obedience to the commands of God, he insists that we cannot think of the will of God as the fundamental principle of morality without transgressing the principle of autonomy; if we help other men merely because we think God has commanded us to, we are implicitly making our supposed moral principle depend on the principle of securing satisfaction or happiness for ourselves. If we say that an action is our duty because God commands it, then to the question 'Why is it our duty to do what God commands?' there can only be two general types of answer. If the answer is 'Because God commands only what is good and right', God's command in itself is clearly not being taken as fundamental; but if the suggestion is that we ought to obey God's command without having any independent ground for believing that it is our duty to obey his commands, our motive for obedience to them, Kant thinks, can in the end only be some form of desire for our own happiness, such as a prudential desire for reward or dislike of punishment.

The supreme principle of morality, then, is the supreme principle of practical reason; and this is the principle of autonomy, which implies that the determining ground of the moral will must be, not any empirical rule or concept, but the formal concept of lawfulness in general, which is a concept of pure reason. Now, even if morality depends on the principle that the will can act in obedience to a law of reason, or of freedom, as opposed to a law of physical necessity, we still need to know how this apparent escape from physical causality is possible. The *Critique of Pure Reason* demonstrated the impossibility of a valid theoretical proof that freedom exists; but if morality presupposes freedom, could it not still be maintained that freedom does not exist and that the whole of morality is consequently an illusion? How do we know that we are justified in taking this step beyond the boundaries of possible sense-experience (for the autonomous will must be a cause which does not itself have a cause preceding it in time—if it did it would not be autonomous—and such an uncaused cause cannot possibly be met with in experience, as the first *Critique* has shown)? Kant's answer is that, although the category of causality, like all the other categories, can give us knowledge only when it is applied to objects met with in actual or possible sense-experience (i.e. to appearances as opposed to things in themselves), the *Critique of Pure Reason* has by no means ruled out as meaningless all non-sensuous application of the categories; in particular, the impossibility of any theoretical application of the categories to noumena in order to gain knowledge of them does not entail the impossibility of their application to noumena in practical contexts for a different purpose. There are two reasons why this is so. First, all the demonstrations in the Dialectic of the first *Critique* that there could be no valid theoretical proof, and hence no knowledge, of the existence of God, freedom, and immortality could serve equally well to demonstrate that there could be no theoretical proof of their non-existence; the possibility of there being rational grounds for accepting or believing in the existence of any or all of these three things is left open. But secondly, when we consider the position of practical, as opposed to theoretical, reason, we are on even firmer ground in our attempt to justify the assumption of freedom. For morality is not an option which we can dismiss as meaningless or illusory if we choose; as long as no theoretical impossibility or contradiction can be exhibited in it or in its presuppositions, morality and its claims must be taken as an inescapable fact—a fact of reason, as it were. The concept of a *causa noumenon*, which is entailed in that of a being with a free will, cannot be given a theoretical justification or deduction, as can that of a *causa phaenomenon*; but it has been shown to be free from contradiction and, since it is itself obviously not an empirical concept, it cannot be maintained that its application must be in all respects and in all contexts limited to objects of possible sense-experience—as long as the application has a practical purpose, that is, is directed to the use of the concept in the establishing of a moral principle, and is not supposed to give us theoretical knowledge, no possible objection can be taken to it.

Through it [sc. the concept of *causa noumenon*] I do not strive to know theoretically the characteristic of a being in so far as it has a pure will; it is enough for me to denote it as such by means of this concept and thus to couple the concept of causality with that of freedom (and with what is inseparable from it, i.e. the moral law as its determining ground). I have this right by virtue of the pure non-empirical origin of the concept of cause, since I here make no other use of the concept than in relation to the moral law which determines its reality; that is, I hold that I am justified only in making a practical use of it. (KPV v 56.)

So far, Kant has argued (i) that morality presupposes autonomy of the will, that is the ability of the will to obey a law which it has imposed on itself as opposed to a law prescribed by some other being, such as God or a political sovereign, and (ii) that the law which is obeyed by the autonomous will (a will which is reason in its practical aspect) must be capable of being shown to be valid because of its purely formal characteristics. Both these theses, however, require further defence and elaboration.

Just how, in the first place, can the claim of autonomy be reconciled with the thesis of universal physical causality? It is not enough to say that the former belongs to man as noumenon, while the latter applies to him only as phenomenon; for this, taken by itself, is more a statement of the problem to be solved than a solution of it. It is an obvious fact, Kant thinks, that respect for the moral law can compete as a rival motive for action with inclinations, appetites, and, in general, incentives that belong to the sphere of feeling. A man may contrast his desire to perform a particular action because he thinks it will conduce to his own happiness with his knowledge that performing it would be contrary to his duty; and if it is his duty to avoid it, it must be possible for him to do so. Now the prima facie difficulty about freedom, Kant thinks, is not that alterations are of necessity causally determined, for there is no reason why an action, as a kind of alteration, should not be determined by an autonomous act of will; the difficulty is that alterations are causally determined by something preceding them in time.

Suppose I say of a man who has committed a theft that this act, by the natural law of causality, is a necessary result of the determining ground existing in the preceding time and that it was therefore impossible that it could not have been done. How, then, can judgement according to the moral law make any change in it? And how can it be supposed that it could still have been left undone because the law says that it should have been left undone? That is, how can he be called free at this point of time with reference to this action, when in this moment and in this action he stands under irrevocable natural necessity? (KPV v 95.)

We cannot solve the problem by suggesting that freedom consists in being determined by one's own desires or feelings, as opposed to those of others, or in being determined by thought rather than by feeling; for as long as the determination is by something, no matter what, which precedes the action in time, it must follow that the action, at the time of its performance, could not have been avoided, its determining causes being outside the agent's control. Psychological causality is as inconsistent with freedom as is mechanical. What is required for morality is the existence of transcendental freedom, that is complete independence of all natural or empirical determination. Now the first *Critique* showed that such independence could not possibly exist within the world of appearances; if it exists at all, therefore, it must belong to man as noumenon, to man as he is in himself. And since noumena do not stand under temporal conditions, the laws of natural necessity cannot apply to them; the temporally ordered actions of man as appearance are causally determined, but the will of man as noumenon is not temporally ordered and therefore the notion of causal necessity simply does not apply to it. Now at first sight this seems absurd, for a man's volitions or decisions, even if they have not yet led or never lead to bodily action, still occur in time; one can put an exact date and time to a decision or to a mental effort just as easily as one can to an intentional physical movement. Kant, however, is not denying anything as obvious as this. What he is saying is that, when we blame or praise a man or hold him accountable for something he has done or tried to do, although his action or volition was a temporal occurrence, it is, as it were, a person considered independently of any temporal considerations whom we are holding responsible. I am the same person that I was ten years ago, in spite of the physical and psychological changes that have taken place in me during that time; as Kant would put it, temporal changes affect the self as phenomenon, but are irrelevant to the self as noumenon. The 'I' that is the object of moral approval or condemnation and to which the moral law applies is the self considered as noumenon: the 'I' whose activities are determined by causal necessity is the self considered as phenomenon. But since the 'I' as noumenon which is condemned if it disobeys the commands of reason expressed in the moral law is a timeless 'I', no one can claim exemption from such condemnation on the ground that his disobedience to the moral law was irresistibly necessitated by some temporally preceding appetite, inclination, or other factor.

From this point of view, a rational being can rightly say of any unlawful action which he has done that he could have left it undone, even if as an appearance it was sufficiently determined in the past and thus far was inescapably necessary. For this action and everything in the past which determined it belong to a single phenomenon of his character, which he himself creates, and according to which he imputes to himself as a cause independent of all sensibility the causality of that appearance. (KPV v 98.)

Even if we knew so much of a man's character that we could infallibly predict his entire future conduct, this would not prove him any the less free; for his character, which leads him to act in these predictable ways, is itself under his control and derives from that spontaneity which he possesses as a noumenon. For the same reason, we are entitled to judge a man guilty of great moral wrongdoing, even after he has become so fixed in his bad habits that he really does have no choice but to act badly; for, assuming that he was free to choose at some earlier stage in his life, he must be held responsible even for his present irresponsibility—the vicious acts spring from his will, considered as a timeless noumenon, since he freely willed the acts which caused his present condition.

Kant, no doubt rightly, had misgivings about the lucidity and intelligibility of this resolution of the supposed conflict between freedom and necessity. He claims that no other solution that has been, or might be, offered is any clearer, and that philosophical difficulties ought to be brought out into the open and not hidden or removed with palliatives, as has been the case with earlier treatments of the problem. But his solution is difficult to accept, as well as difficult to understand, for it does not seem to meet the requirements for a solution which Kant himself lays down. Suppose that I am wondering whether to pay back a loan from a friend as I have promised, or to spend the money on my own entertainment. It is clear that I can pay back the loan and that I can, in exactly the same sense, spend the money on myself. Suppose now that after long consideration I yield to temptation and spend it on myself. Kant, as a moralist, will say, 'You ought not to have done that' and also 'You could have refrained from doing that'. But as a metaphysician, believing in the universal applicability of causal necessity to events and thus to actions, he will also say 'Your doing what you did was causally necessitated, and therefore you could not have done otherwise'. There is an apparent contradiction here between two different statements about the same action, considered as a temporal occurrence; and it is not clear how reference to the timelessness of man as an intelligible being or noumenon can remove it.

Kant would, I think, have dealt with any objections to his attempted solution of the problem of freedom and its reconciliation with universal causal necessity by saying that since freedom is required by morality and causal necessity by metaphysics or philosophy of science, there must be some way of reconciling the apparent contradiction between them, even if that way has not yet been discovered. Of course, if there were a real contradiction, belief in freedom would have to be given up (that Kant would have chosen this horn of the dilemma is made clear in the *Grundlegung* IV 456); but the *Critique of Pure Reason* showed at least that the supposition of freedom does not of itself lead to theoretical contradictions, and we should be justified in abandoning freedom, and with it morality, only if it could be proved to be in contradiction either with itself or with any other firmly established principles. The discovery of the distinction between man as noumenon in the intelligible world and man as appearance in the sensible world, Kant would say, at least gives us some ground for holding that the apparent conflict arises from previous failures to grasp the distinction, even if a clear and precise explanation of the difficulty has not yet been achieved.

I shall defer for the moment an account of the way in which the nature and content of the moral law is connected by Kant with the formal characteristics of the rational will, and deal briefly with some topics discussed in the second part of the *Critique of Practical Reason*, the Dialectic. Practical reason, like speculative, has its natural dialectic; that is, it is involved in illusion or contradiction through its inevitable attempt to find the unconditional principle of everything that is conditioned—here the categorical moral principle or law which stands over and above all the lower-order, conditioned principles, based as they are on inclinations. Practical reason tries to find a law which men must obey unconditionally as opposed to a collection of rules which they need to obey only on condition that they want to achieve their own happiness, or some other less extensive end. The task then is to define the concept of the highest good, in the light of which the conditioned goodness of all other good things must be judged. As Kant puts it in the well-known words at the beginning of the first chapter of the *Grundlegung*, 'It is impossible to conceive anything at all in the world, or even out of it, which can be taken without qualification as good, except a good will' (IV 393). Kant goes on there to say that other qualities of mind or temperament such as intelligence and courage, and gifts of fortune such as wealth or health, though they are good and desirable in many ways, can also at times be bad and hurtful, and that the test of their goodness is the goodness of the will which controls or employs them.

Now the phrase 'the highest good' (*summum bonum*) is, Kant says, ambiguous. It can mean either the supreme good (*bonum supremum*) or the complete or perfect good (*bonum consummatum*). The former is the unconditioned condition, viz. the good will, or virtue, to which all human action must be subordinate. But although a man's possession of moral virtue is a necessary condition of the complete goodness of his state or situation, it is not a sufficient condition; the concept of virtue carries with it the concept of worthiness to be happy, and it is impossible for a rational being to approve of a situation in which a being who needs happiness and deserves it should nevertheless be unhappy. The complete good (*bonum consummatum*) consists then in virtue together with happiness in due proportion to virtue. Now the question arises as to the nature of the relation between virtue and happiness. It is clearly a synthetic connexion, not an analytic one: to be happy is not necessarily to be virtuous, nor does the possession of virtue carry happiness with it as a logical necessity. But given that it is a synthetic connexion, either the desire for happiness must be the motive for virtuous conduct or the maxim of virtue must necessarily produce happiness. Yet neither of these alternatives seems in fact to be true (hence the antinomy of practical reason). For the Analytic has shown that to subordinate moral considerations to the desire for happiness is to destroy morality entirely, because of the consequent violation of the principle of autonomy: while, since a man's happiness depends at least in part on factors outside the control of his own will and determined by ordinary physical laws of nature, it cannot be expected that the pursuit of virtue will always in fact bring a man happiness, however much he may deserve it.

Kant says that the resolution of this antinomy resembles that of the antinomies of speculative reason which were dealt with in the Transcendental Dialectic of the first *Critique*. The resemblance is only partial, however; for in the earlier work, once the distinction between things in themselves and appearances had been introduced, both the thesis and the antithesis of each antinomy were seen to be on a par with one another, in two cases both false, and in two cases both true. Here, however, the first alternative is firmly and unconditionally rejected; there is no sense in which the search for happiness can provide a rational expectation of attaining virtue. The objection to the second alternative, on the other hand, can be removed, Kant thinks, if we apply it to man as noumenon rather than to man as appearance. Under conditions pertaining in the physical world of appearance it is indeed untrue to say that a virtuous disposition necessarily produces happiness; but to suppose that this is the last word is to mistake a mere relation between appearances (between the happiness of a man considered as appearance—i.e. the satisfaction of his appetites and inclinations—and the physical conditions of that happiness, which belong only to the world of phenomena) for a relation between things in themselves and appearances. Man *qua* noumenon is not subject to the changes and chances of the physical world; and it is to man *qua* noumenon that morality, and the consequential worthiness to be happy, pertain.

Speculative reason could not prove either the immortality of the soul or the existence of God, although the possibility that these propositions are none the less true was left open by the conclusions of the first *Critique*. But the problem raised by the concept of the highest good can be solved only on the assumption that they are true; in other words, they are both postulates of pure practical reason. We are commanded by the moral law to achieve the highest good possible in the world. But the complete assimilation of the will to the moral law is holiness, a state which is not attainable in the world of sense (a holy will, unlike a human will, cannot be tempted by inclination or appetite to disobey the moral law). Since, however, holiness is both required by the moral law and impossible in this physical existence, its possibility requires the possibility of a different, non-physical existence in which the moral development of a will can reach perfection. 'Thus the highest good is practically possible only on the supposition of the immortality of the soul, and the latter, as inseparably bound to the moral law, is a postulate of practical reason' (KPV v 122).

Just as the problem presented by the place of the concept of morality in that of the highest good could be solved only by postulating immortality, so, Kant thinks, that presented by the requirement that happiness should be attained in proportion to virtue can be solved only by postulating the existence of God. A man is not the cause of nature and his will is therefore unable to ensure that nature metes out the happiness which through his virtue he deserves, or the unhappiness which he might deserve through vice. But the existence of a connexion between virtue and deserved happiness is postulated as necessary by the moral law and its requirement that we should seek to further the highest good; it follows that the moral law also postulates the existence of a supreme cause of nature which can bring about the required correspondence of virtue and morality which would otherwise not exist, i.e. it is morally necessary to assume the existence of God.

Thus the immortality of the soul and the existence of God have been shown, like the freedom of the will, to be presupposed by morality. The propositions which could not be proved by speculative metaphysics have still not been proved; but, Kant thinks, it has been shown that we may rationally believe them, since without them morality, or at least the concept of the highest good which morality bids us achieve, would be impossible. The concepts of God, freedom, and immortality belong in the end not to metaphysics but to morality:

> Granted that the pure moral law inexorably binds every man as a command (not as a rule of prudence), the righteous man may say: I will that there be a God, that my existence in this world be also an existence in a pure world of the understanding outside the system of natural connections, and finally that my duration be endless. (KPV v 143.)

The existence of a need based on inclination does not, of course, entail the existence of an object which can satisfy that need; but the existence of God, freedom, and immortality are postulated because of a need for them which is based on practical reason, not on inclination, and a need of reason, Kant holds, cannot remain unsatisfied.

Kant's treatment of these last two postulates is brief and, even by his own standards of difficulty, hard to follow. It is not easy to see, for example, why an obligation to pursue the highest good need presuppose the possibility, in some existence or other, of achieving it. Could we not regard the highest good, however it is defined, as an ideal of morality, to which we are required to approach as closely as our own abilities and the restrictions placed on our activity by the conditions of our physical existence allow? Again, Kant seems to take it for granted that there is something radically unsatisfactory about a distribution of happiness that is not directly proportional to virtue. But, apart from the difficulty of establishing a proportion between two such disparate concepts as virtue and happiness, it would be interesting to have some rational argument for this thesis, however obvious its truth appeared to Kant; is it really so obvious that the world is an unsatisfactory place if it contains a not very good man who is very happy, and that it would become less unsatisfactory if he were to be made unhappy instead? There are often, no doubt, reasons why it is expedient that the wicked should suffer for their wickedness and the virtuous be rewarded for their virtue—reasons connected with the desirability of discouraging vice and encouraging virtue; but Kant treats the connexion between virtue and happiness as self-evident, not as a matter of expediency.

We must now turn to examine the relation between the basic principle of Kant's moral philosophy and the lower-order principles, rules, and judgements which accord with this principle. The principle of universality, which we may take as our starting-point, enables us to express the categorical imperative of morality in its most abstract form: 'Act only on that maxim through which you can at the same time will that it should become a universal law' (*Grundlegung* IV 421). Kant's systematic exposition of the various different types of moral prescription or duty as exemplifications of this formula is found in the *Metaphysic of Morals*. Some important remarks on this subject, however, are to be found in the *Critique of Practical Reason* and, more especially, in the *Grundlegung*, and these deserve some preliminary attention.

It is easy, Kant says at one point in the *Critique of Practical Reason*, to distinguish the formal quality of a maxim which makes it suitable or unsuitable as the case may be for universal lawgiving. Suppose I have in my possession some property which has been deposited with me by its owner, who has subsequently died without leaving any record or informing anyone else of it; and suppose that I have adopted the maxim (the personal, subjective rule of conduct) of increasing my property by every safe means.

Now I want to know whether this maxim can hold also as a universal practical law. I apply it, therefore, to the present case and ask if it could take the form of a law, and consequently whether I could, by the maxim, make the law that every man is allowed to deny that a deposit has been made when no one can prove the contrary. I immediately realize that taking such a principle as a law would annihilate itself, because its result would be that no one would make such a deposit. (KPV v 27.)

Kant does not discuss this example at any great length, and the brevity of his treatment has often led to misunderstanding. He is not, as some have suggested, putting forward a disguised form of utilitarianism; i.e. he is not saying 'If there were such a universal law, no one would make deposits of this kind; but this would be a bad or undesirable state of affairs; therefore, there should not, or could not, be such a universal law'. His point is, rather, that the man who holds on to a deposit in such circumstances is behaving irrationally because (i) if his own maxim is to be a rational one, it must be possible to will a universal law that everyone should act in the same way and (ii) a universal law to the effect that everyone may deny that a deposit has been made when there is no record of it would not serve the purpose it is intended to serve (viz. that of safely enriching the agent), for if there were such a law, deposits of this kind would never be made. No one would perform an immoral act of this kind if he did not think that he would gain some advantage from it; but the universal permissibility of the act would ensure that the hoped-for advantage would never result.

The other moral examples in the second *Critique* receive equally cursory treatment, though there is one feature which requires mention. Instead of asking whether a certain maxim could hold as a universal law, Kant now asks whether it could hold as a universal law of nature. The addition of the reference to nature does not affect the general principles of his argument; the law of nature is regarded as a type or analogue of the moral law, and its introduction serves the purpose of making the relevant question (Could one will that this maxim should become a universal law?) easier to answer, because we now have something more concrete to consider.

The rule of judgement under laws of pure practical reason is: Ask yourself whether, if the action which you propose should take place by a law of nature of which you were yourself a part, you could regard it as possible through your will. Everyone does, in fact, decide by this rule whether actions are morally good or bad. Thus people ask: If one belonged to such an order of things that anyone would allow himself to deceive when he thought it to his advantage, or felt justified in shortening his life as soon as he was thoroughly weary of it, or looked with complete indifference on the needs of others, would he assent of his own will to being a member of such an order of things? (KPV v 69.)

It is clear, Kant thinks, that a negative answer would have to be given in all three cases. Truthfulness is morally required of us for a reason similar to that offered in the deposit example; suicide through weariness of life is wrong because no permanent natural order could be constituted in which any member was entitled to put an arbitrary end to his life; and no system would be tolerable to reason in which individual members needed, but could not rely on receiving, help from others. Since there is scarcely anything here in the way of argument, there is no point in discussing the moral examples of the *Critique of Practical Reason* in any further detail.

There is something to be said, however, about the examples in the *Grundlegung*, where the discussion is rather less sketchy and a good deal more systematic. The system, however, according to which various types of duty are divided is not one to which Kant attaches any great importance; he says that he will reserve his method of classifying duties for the *Metaphysic of Morals*, which had yet to be written, and this later method differs in some respects, as we shall see, from the provisional one of the *Grundlegung*. Following a twofold distinction, that between duties to oneself and duties to others, and that between perfect[1] and imperfect duties, Kant discusses four examples. The first is of a perfect duty to oneself. A man contemplating suicide as a result of great misfortune asks himself whether his maxim ('From self-love I make it my principle to shorten my life if its continuance threatens more evil than it promises pleasure') can become a universal law of nature. The answer, Kant says, is clearly that it cannot; for a contradiction would arise if in one system of nature the feeling (self-love) whose function it is to prolong and preserve life were at the same time to promote its destruction. The second example is of a perfect duty to others. A man in need of money wonders whether to borrow some on a promise (which he knows he will not be able to keep) to pay it back within a certain time. His maxim ('Whenever I believe myself short of money, I will borrow money and promise to pay it back, though I know that this will never be done') cannot become a universal law of nature, for it would, if put in universal form, contradict itself.

For the universality of a law that everyone believing himself to be in need can make any promise he pleases with the intention of breaking it would make

[1] A perfect duty, unlike an imperfect one, allows of no exceptions in the interests of inclination. It is my duty to keep all my promises, whatever I may feel like doing; but since I cannot develop all my talents or help every man in distress, I have some latitude in deciding which talents to develop and which men to help.

promising, and the very purpose of promising, itself impossible, since no one
would believe he was being promised anything, but would laugh at utterances of
this kind as empty shams. (*Grundlegung* IV 422.)

The third and fourth examples (of imperfect duty to oneself and to
others, respectively) differ in an important respect from the first two.
There the notion that a law of nature which embodied the universalized
form of the relevant maxim could exist was said to involve a contradiction: now, although the maxim could exist as a universal law of nature,
it is impossible for anyone to will its existence. Suppose, in the third
example, a man who is reluctant to take the trouble necessary to develop
some useful talent which he possesses, and who prefers a life of pleasure.
A system of nature based on the universalization of the maxim of neglect-
ing one's natural gifts would not be self-defeating nor, by itself, give rise
to any self-contradiction; nevertheless it is not a possible object of a
rational will. Such a man

sees that a system of nature could indeed always subsist under such a universal
law. . . . Only he cannot possibly *will* that this should become a universal law of
nature or should be implanted in us as such a law by a natural instinct. For as a
rational being he necessarily wills that all his powers should be developed, since
they serve him, and are given him, for possible ends of all kinds. (*Grundlegung*
IV 423.)

Fourthly and finally, a man wonders whether it is not morally permissible to refrain from helping others who are in need or distress, as
long as he does not, inconsistently, demand help from others. A state
of affairs in which no one helped anyone else is theoretically possible, but
it is impossible to will that a universal law of nature should exist according to which no help was ever given to people in need;

for a will which decided in this way would be at variance with itself, since many
a situation might arise in which the man needed love and sympathy from others,
and in which, by such a law of nature sprung from his own will, he would rob
himself of all hope of the help he wants for himself. (*Grundlegung* IV 423.)

This last is not intended by Kant as a prudential argument. He is not saying that a man had better help others in need in order that he may receive
help from them in his turn, but that it is inconsistent and irrational to
refuse to help others if you are going sooner or later to need and expect
help from them.

In general, Kant notes as an addendum to his discussion of these four
examples, a man who wills or acts wrongly does not will that his morally
bad maxim should become a universal law, but that the universal moral

law should remain in force while he, exceptionally, is allowed to transgress it; moral wrongdoing implies a contradiction or inconsistency in the will of the wrongdoer.

Kant proceeds to restate his objections to the moral wrongdoing illustrated in his examples in a number of different ways: the categorical imperative which prescribes conduct according to maxims which can at the same time be willed as universal laws of nature can also be formulated as prescribing that we treat humanity, whether in our own person or in that of others, always as an end, and never simply as a means, and this leads Kant to the concept of a kingdom of ends—a society of rational beings each obeying a common law, but a law which he has imposed on himself, in accordance with the principle of autonomy.

Because the *Grundlegung* has always been one of Kant's most frequently studied works (partly, no doubt, because of its brevity), there has been a regrettable tendency to treat it as containing everything, or almost everything, of importance that Kant wished to say about moral philosophy, apart from the highly abstruse epistemological theses of the *Critique of Practical Reason* itself. This approach is explicitly contradicted by Kant himself in the preface to the *Grundlegung*, where he discusses the purpose of the work quite clearly and unambiguously. He is not yet ready, he says (IV 391), to proceed to a full Critique of Practical Reason, which would 'show the unity of practical and theoretical reason in a common principle'; on the other hand, he is not writing a Metaphysic of Morals, but is discussing only the foundations for such an enterprise. He is not saying everything he has to say about the relation between the fundamental principle of morality and particular, lower-order, moral principles; and the concrete examples which we have discussed are examples designed to explain the meaning of the fundamental principle rather than part of a systematic attempt to explain the working-out of that principle in moral practice. This systematic attempt is reserved for the *Metaphysic of Morals*.

Before we consider this work, however, two points arise out of what Kant has said so far. The first concerns his suggestion that a great deal of moral wrong-doing involves the agent in an attempt to make an exception in his own interest to a rule which, as applied to other agents, he accepts. This is no doubt true; but Kant seems to exaggerate the scope and importance of this kind of inconsistency. A man who refuses to help others when they are in need acts irrationally and inconsistently, he holds, because there will inevitably be occasions on which he will need help from others, and yet the universal adoption of his way of acting would deprive him of this help. In other words, such a man does not really accept a world in which no one received help when he needed it; what happens is that he accepts the general principle that men should help one another but fails to live up to it himself. Now although behaviour of this kind is admittedly inconsistent and wrong, the reduction of a refusal to help those in need to a formal inconsistency is, to say the least, an over-simplification. It can hardly be maintained that this is the only reason why we ought to help others, even if it is one reason. For one thing, if Kant were right, no one would be morally obliged to give more help than he expects to receive from others; and if there were, *per impossibile*, a man who needed no help, Kant would have to admit that he had no duty to help others—but if suffering and death are evils, as they are held to be by moralists of all kinds, it is hard to see why everyone should not have some obligation to reduce or remove them, however invulnerable he might be himself.

The second point concerns Kant's deliberate concentration on formal elements in such cases as the deposit and the false promise. One could without much difficulty construct examples formally parallel to Kant's which would lead to moral conclusions of a paradoxical kind. If it can be shown on purely formal grounds that it is wrong to break a promise for reasons of pleasure or convenience, or to make a promise one does not intend to keep, then it can likewise be shown that it is wrong to fail for the same reasons to fulfil a threat or to make a threat one does not intend to carry out. Yet it is by no means obvious that it is always wrong to act in either of these ways; but the difference between threats and promises, which leads naturally to our drawing different moral conclusions in the two cases, is not, in the Kantian sense, a formal difference at all. What Kant seems to overlook in his treatment of the false promise example is that the keeping of a promise is normally of benefit either to the promisee or to someone in whose welfare the promisee is interested. Making a promise which one does not intend to keep may involve some kind of contradiction or inconsistency in the will, as Kant maintains; but it is morally wrong partly, at least, because it leads the promisee to expect some benefit, direct or indirect, which the promisor has in fact no inten-tion of providing. If the expectation were of a harmful or neutral action, the morality of the situation would be quite different.

The *Metaphysic of Morals*, although it was envisaged by Kant when he wrote the *Grundlegung*, was not written until much later (it was published in 1797, when he was seventy-three). It is in some ways an unsatisfactory work, and the fact that it is a composition of Kant's old age may help in part at least to explain why. He had for some time been complaining in letters to his friends that he was feeling his age and was no longer as capable as he had been of engaging in difficult abstract thought. We might well expect to find, and indeed we clearly do find, some signs of this deterioration in the *Metaphysic of Morals* and other works of this period. Because of this, my treatment of the work will contain a somewhat higher proportion of criticism than is to be found elsewhere in this book; most of this criticism, however, is made as far as possible from within Kant's own general philosophical position. Purely external criticism I have tried here, as elsewhere, to avoid.

The *Metaphysic of Morals* is divided into two parts, the '*Metaphysische Anfangsgründe der Rechtslehre*' ('Metaphysical Elements of Justice') and the '*Metaphysische Anfangsgründe der Tugendlehre*' ('Metaphysical Elements of Virtue'). It is a work of metaphysics, in Kant's own sense of the word; that is, it is not speculative metaphysics but attempts to explain and establish the principles of morality by a priori methods, without drawing on any empirical knowledge of human nature (which Kant calls 'anthropology'). There is a parallel here, to which Kant himself calls attention, with his earlier *Metaphysische Anfangsgründe der Naturwissenschaft* (published in 1786), which dealt with the a priori principles of physics, i.e. with principles which are not tested or testable by the experiments of scientists but which are presupposed by all scientific observation and thinking. These metaphysical essays form a halfway house, so to speak, between empirical generalizations about the behaviour of matter or the conduct of human beings on the one hand and the examination of the functions and limitations of reason which we find in the first two *Critiques* on the other.

It is not, on the whole, Kant's purpose in the *Metaphysic of Morals* to give reasoned advice to his readers as to how they ought to live, even though he cannot resist talking on occasions as if it were; his considered view is that the ordinary well-intentioned man knows quite well without the aid of philosophy what he ought to do. His is not an applied ethics in the sense of a manual of moral precepts; he sometimes lists casuistical questions, but rarely answers them. His main purpose is to establish the a priori principles of morality which apply, not merely in the abstract to all rational beings qua rational, but to all men as men. For their detailed application these principles require a systematic study of human nature (anthropology), although they cannot themselves be derived from anthropological sources. The application of moral principles which can be discussed in the *Metaphysic of Morals* is of a general kind, and does not take into account any racial, national, or individual differences between men.

Both parts of the *Metaphysic of Morals* are concerned with what Kant calls laws of freedom (as opposed to laws of nature, which determine the behaviour of physical objects); these are moral laws which prescribe the use man ought to make of his freedom of choice.

In so far as they [moral laws] are directed to mere external actions and their legality (*Gesetzmässigkeit*), they are called juridical (*juridisch*) but when, in addition, they demand that these laws be the determining grounds of actions, then they are ethical (*ethisch*). Accordingly we say: agreement with juridical laws constitutes the legality (*Legalität*) of action, whereas agreement with ethical ones constitutes its morality (*Moralität*). (MdS vi 214.)

The English word 'legality' is liable to mislead here, suggesting as it does conformity with the law of the land; Kant, however, means conformity with the moral law, and the distinction between *Legalität* or *Gesetz-mässigkeit* on the one hand and *Moralität* on the other is a more technical-sounding version of that, already familiar to readers of the *Grundlegung*, between action in accordance with duty and action from duty (between action that is correct according to the rules of morality and action which is performed with respect for those rules as its motive). The first part of the distinction is concerned with the question Is action X right or wrong, just or unjust? and an action, in Kant's view, can be right or wrong what-ever its motive or maxim may have been. I am acting rightly or justly when I repay a debt, even if I repay it only in the hope that my creditor, whom I hate, will drink himself to death on whisky bought with the money; and I am acting wrongly or unjustly if I refrain from paying the debt on the agreed date through forgetfulness or in the genuine belief that repayment was not due for another month—i.e. it is not necessary that I should intend to neglect a duty of justice before I can properly be held to have neglected it. The second part of the distinction is concerned with the question Was action Y performed from a moral motive (i.e. Does it have moral worth in addition to being morally right or just?)? Kant is reluctant to accept the possibility that an act which was performed simply because the agent believed it was his duty to perform it might nevertheless be morally wrong or unjust; but it is clearly possible, even on his own principles—for a man who is trying to obey for its own sake the legal, as opposed to the ethical, version of the Categorical Imperative ('Act externally in such a way that the free use of your will is compatible with the freedom of everyone according to a universal law' (MdS vi 231)) may believe that his action is thus compatible when in fact it is not. The application of the Categorical Imperative, Kant tells us (*Grundlegung* iv 389), requires the use of judgement in addition to a knowledge of the

to transgress one's own rights, as it is to respect or to transgress the rights of others.

The second difficulty is that, whatever one may think of the nature of Kant's distinction between duties to oneself and duties to others, the first of his two categories contains some surprising members. One would think that a paradigm case of a duty to others would be the duty of truth-telling; if I tell a lie without justification (Kant did not, in fact, believe that there could be any justification for lying), then I do not merely act wrongly, I act wrongly towards the person to whom I tell the lie, and he has a right to complain about my conduct. Yet, for Kant, lying is a violation of duty to oneself, indeed the most serious of such violations. Lying is accompanied by dishonour in the eyes of others, and by shame in one's own: 'By a lie a man throws away and, as it were, annihilates his dignity as a man. A man who himself does not believe what he tells another . . . has even less worth than if he were a mere thing' (MdS VI 428). (The argument seems to be that a thing has some use, whereas a man, to the extent that he is lying, is of no use to anyone; but what if he is lying in order to help someone else? Would his lying not be useful, even if it was wrong?) One of the objections to this passage is obvious, namely that Kant is dogmatically putting forward a strong personal opinion concerning a moral issue as though it were a reasoned philosophical principle— a practice which is regrettably common in the *Metaphysic of Morals* and of which many more examples could be given. Kant is apt throughout this work to forget his own insistence that moral feeling should be subordinate to the thought of the moral law, and that it is for the judgement of reason to validate or criticize feeling, not for feeling to support or oppose reason. Many of the moral rules which Kant claims to derive from his metaphysical principles are not validly derived; and with many of them, indeed, there is hardly any attempt at reasoned derivation. A second objection is more specific, and concerns Kant's use of the concept of self-respect, which is central to his treatment of duties to oneself. Whatever the purpose for which a man tells a lie, Kant says, his decision to use this way of achieving his end 'is, by its mere form, a wrong to his own person and a baseness which must make him contemptible in his own eyes' (MdS VI 428). Now in spite of this dogmatic insistence that lying must make a man contemptible in his own eyes, it is clear that sometimes, with some men, it does not have this effect. There is, however, a more serious objection than this disregard of plain fact. What Kant overlooks is that, to the extent that one's moral judging is rational (and Kant's, above all, claims to be this) one's feeling of shame or loss of self-respect is a valid indication that one has acted wrongly only if the action of which one is ashamed is wrong antecedently to the fact that one is ashamed of it. I may feel ashamed of lying if I think that I ought not to have lied, and lying is, of course, in general wrong; but the fact that one feels ashamed of an action is not conclusive evidence that it was wrong. For it is quite possible to feel ashamed of actions which are not wrong, but which one has been led or trained to believe wrong; a young man who has been brought up as a strict teetotaller may feel ashamed after he has drunk his nrst pint of beer, but he has not done anything to be ashamed of. Whatever, then, may be the reason why lying is wrong, it cannot be because it evinces lack of self-respect or because a man feels ashamed after he has told a lie.

Kant could perhaps retort that he is not relying on the concepts of shame or self-respect alone; for there is, he thinks, a further reason why the man whose conduct makes him ashamed or fails to evince self-respect is acting improperly. 'Man as a moral being (*homo noumenon*) cannot use his natural being (*homo phaenomenon*) as a mere means (a speaking machine), as if it were not bound to its intrinsic end (the communication of thought)' (MdS VI 429). In other words, lying is wrong because the liar is using one of his natural capacities in a way or for a purpose contrary to that assigned to it by nature. And Kant uses teleological or purposive arguments of this kind in many other contexts besides that of lying: it is wrong, for example, to commit suicide because this is 'to abase humanity in one's own person, which was yet entrusted to man for its preservation' (MdS VI 422), and beneficence towards the needy is a duty 'because men are to be considered fellow-men—that is, rational beings with needs, united by nature in one dwelling-place for the purpose of helping one another' (MdS VI 452). Now the argument that, because some capacity has been given us by nature for a certain purpose, it is wrong either to use it for a different purpose which conflicts with the first one or not to use it at all is in itself a dubious moral argument; it is not clear how the original claim of the purposiveness of nature could be substantiated nor, if it could, how it could be proved that the thwarting of this purposiveness is morally wrong without first substantiating the moral claim which is supposed to follow from its being thwarted. And Kant certainly provides no argument to show that either of these things is possible. But the argument is not only dubious and question-begging in itself, it is also at variance with two of Kant's own most fundamental philosophical theses, the principle of autonomy and the view that the purposiveness of nature is a regulative, and not a constitutive, principle of reason. If some faculty or capacity has been given me by nature, or by God, or anyone else for a particular purpose, it cannot for this reason alone be my duty to use it for this purpose and no other; for if it could, my will would then be subordinate to the will of God or to the 'will' of nature—that is, it would cease to be autonomous and thus cease to be a moral will. As to the purposiveness of nature, it is, as we shall see,[1] one of the most important theses of the *Critique of Judgement* that the attribution of purpose, in some sense of the word, to nature is not to be taken as an objective fact about nature, but as an assumption which we, because of the limitations of our human intellects, must make if we are to achieve any scientific understanding of nature, and in particular of plant and animal life. It is still conceivable, Kant thinks, that a superhuman understanding could explain the whole of nature as a product of straightforward causal laws.

When teleology is applied to physics, we speak with perfect justice of the wisdom, the economy, the forethought, the beneficence of nature. But in so doing we do not convert nature into an intelligent being, for that would be absurd; but neither do we dare to think of placing another being, one that is intelligent, above nature as its architect, for that would be presumptuous. On the contrary our only intention is to designate in this way a kind of natural causality on an analogy with our own causality in the technical employment of reason, for the purpose of keeping in view the rule upon which certain natural products are to be investigated. (KU v 383.)

We cannot assert that nature *is* purposive, although we cannot understand nature unless we investigate her as if she were. But no moral conclusions can be validly derived from an 'as if' proposition of this kind.

It might be thought that the morally irrelevant introduction of the concept of objective purposiveness is an accidental excrescence, as it were, and that the same moral point might have been made in a less objectionable way; but the difficulty is not so easily resolved. We might, admittedly, doubt the objectivity of the statement that the purpose of the heart is to circulate blood through the body, and yet be content with the plain statement that if the heart stops beating the blood stops circulating. But from an analogous translation of statements about the purpose of nature in giving man his various instincts and capacities, the required moral conclusions do not follow. Instead, for example, of saying, with Kant, that man has been given the power of speech for the purpose of communicating his thoughts, and that the use of it to conceal his thoughts or to deceive is therefore wrong, we could say only that if all men tell lies

---

[1] See especially pp. 112-18 below.

indiscriminately they will not be able to communicate their thoughts; but even if this is true, no moral conclusion to the wrongness of lying follows unless we assume that the communication of thoughts is a good thing, and the impossibility of communication bad. All Kant's statements, in fact, to the effect that man has been given this or that capacity for this or that purpose are disguised ways of saying or implying that the purposes in question are good; and the goodness of these purposes must be proved, not assumed, if the moral conclusion is to be rational.

The field of jurisprudence, or the science of right or justice,[1] which is the topic of the first part of the *Metaphysic of Morals* but about which little has so far been said, consists in all those laws which can be enacted as external legislation, that is as laws which prescribe actions, as opposed to maxims for action. A man is morally good to the extent that his will is good, even if on occasion his good will fails, through no fault of his own, to translate itself into action; but jurisprudence or the science of right is concerned with laws which require certain things to be done—a morally good intention is neither a necessary nor a sufficient condition for the lawfulness of an action, even though it may be so for its morality. The laws of jurisprudence are nevertheless still laws of freedom; that is, they concern behaviour only in so far as it is free and under the control of the agent. In referring to laws of this kind Kant is not, of course, speaking of the actual positive laws of any existing state; he is referring to conditions which such positive laws must fulfil if they are to deserve the name of law instead, for example, of being merely arbitrary instructions of a tyrant or of a despotic government.

The fundamental universal principle of justice, Kant thinks, can be derived from three simple considerations. First, justice is concerned with those relationships in which one man can, by his conduct, influence the well-being or, in general, the condition, of another; a man can be just or unjust only in his behaviour to others. Secondly, the concept of justice has nothing to do with the relation between the will of one man and the wishes or needs of another (i.e. laws of justice do not prescribe acts of benevolence or charity), but concerns only a relation between one man's will and the will of another. It concerns, in short, those intentional actions which may affect the power of others to act according to their choice. Thirdly, justice concerns only the form of the will, not its matter;

[1] There is no exact English equivalent of the German noun *Recht*; it means something like justice or right or law in the abstract, and must be distinguished from *Gesetz*, which refers to a concrete, enacted law.

in assessing whether an action is just or unjust we ignore such questions as whether it will help the agent to achieve some objective of his, such as personal profit, and inquire only into its formal properties. Justice then, Kant concludes, is the sum total of the conditions under which one person's will can be united with another's under a universal law of freedom; and the universal law of justice, corresponding to the Categorical Imperative of morality, is 'Act externally in such a way that the free use of your will[1] is compatible with the freedom of everyone according to a universal law' (MdS VI 231). Kant insists that, although this is the fundamental principle of justice, justice itself does not require that we adopt it as a maxim. As long as I do not in fact infringe a man's freedom, it is not unjust of me to be indifferent to his freedom or even to desire to infringe it; these last attitudes, as indications of volition not expressed in outward behaviour, may well be morally wrong, but they are not unjust.

Since injustice is the arbitrary imposing of constraints on the freedom of another, constraint is legitimate, in Kant's view, in order to prevent unjust acts; men may be compelled to act justly because it is legitimate to prevent hindrances to freedom. Hence a universal law which at once prescribes rules of justice and lays down sanctions against their non-observance is a law which promotes, rather than destroys or limits, freedom.

When it is said that a creditor has a right to demand from his debtor the payment of a debt, this does not mean that he can persuade the debtor that his own reason itself obligates him to this performance; on the contrary, to say that he has such a right means only that the use of coercion to make anyone do this is entirely compatible with everyone's freedom, including the freedom of the debtor, in accordance with universal laws. (MdS VI 232.)

Freedom is thus man's sole innate right, a right which belongs to him solely in virtue of his humanity. (The right to equality is not, as some have thought, an independent basic human right, but is derivable from

---

[1] In his latest writings on moral questions Kant introduces a technical distinction which is not found in the *Critique of Practical Reason* or the *Grundlegung*, that between *Wille* and *Willkür*. The distinction is not easy to render in translation, since 'will' is usually the nearest English equivalent for both. *Wille* is the rational will, practical reason, regarded as the source of laws of freedom, both ethical and legal: *Willkür* is the individual will, regarded as the author or source of each particular choice or act of volition. *Wille* is neither free nor unfree, since it issues in laws, not actions: *Willkür* is free or unfree according as it is immune from, or subject to, constraint (cf. MdS VI 226). Hence 'will', in such passages as the present one, always translates *Willkür*, not *Wille*.

the right to freedom; it is equivalent to the right not to be constrained by others to a greater extent than that to which one is entitled to constrain them.)

Law has two divisions, private and public. Kant does not say much about private law, but some of his remarks are important. They are mostly concerned with the concept of property. The distinction between having an object in one's physical possession and being the legal owner of it. is linked with the distinction between phenomena and noumena. It is an empirical question whether a particular object is in my physical possession or not; the question can be answered by looking to see whether the object is in my hands, or on my person, or in my house or, in general, in some sufficiently close physical relationship to myself, and possession of this kind is called by Kant *possessio phaenomenon*. Legal ownership cannot be tested in this way, however, for a thing may be in my physical possession even if I do not own it, and vice versa; an object is mine legally if it is so connected with me that anyone who uses it without my consent thereby does me an injury. Legal ownership, since it can only be defined by means of a rational concept (the concept of injury or injustice), is called *possessio noumenon* or intelligible possession.

Legal ownership ('an external mine and thine') can exist, Kant insists, only in civil society. The mere declaration that something is mine cannot make it mine by right; for my legal ownership of something implies an obligation on others to refrain from using it without my consent, and no mere fiat of mine can create such an obligation—any attempt to impose such a fiat would be an arbitrary and therefore unjust interference with their freedom. If we do speak of a man's property rights in a state of nature, Kant says, these rights must be thought of as provisional and as subject to the presumption that they will eventually be confirmed by the entry of the individuals concerned into a civil society.

Public law concerns the laws that must be promulgated and enforced in a civil society or group of such societies; in the first case it is municipal law (*Staatsrecht*), in the second international law (*Völkerrecht*). The law of a state must spring from a will which is thought of as the collective will of the community; legislative power thus belongs to the people. This does not mean, however, that all members of a state have full voting and deliberative rights. A subject is not qualified to be a citizen in the fullest sense (an active as opposed to a passive citizen, to use Kant's terminology) if he possesses an inferior social status which denies him the right to control the behaviour of others as much as they can control his. Apprentices, private servants, women and children, and

in general all those who depend for their subsistence on their sub-
ordination to others, can be citizens in the passive sense only; independent workmen and state employees, on the other hand, are free from
personal subservience and are therefore active citizens.

> The woodcutter whom I employ on my estate; the smith in India who goes
> with his hammer, anvil, and bellows into houses to work on iron, in contrast to
> the European carpenter or smith, who can offer the products of his labour for
> public sale; the private tutor, in contrast to the schoolteacher; the sharecropper,
> in contrast to the farmer; and the like—all are mere underlings of the common-
> wealth, because they must be under the orders or protection of other individuals.
> Consequently, they do not possess any civil independence. (MdS vi 314-15.)

As an explanation of the politically inferior position in some existing
eighteenth-century societies of those whose social status implied personal service to another, this is straightforward enough; but like other
a priori arguments in the *Metaphysic of Morals* for permanent moral and
legal conclusions it is too cursorily stated and makes too many assumptions to be able to fulfil its intended function. The whole argument,
indeed, might be turned on its head: since existing political and social
conditions make it impossible for private servants to exercise the full
rights of citizenship, this indicates clearly the injustice of those conditions, which prevent the equal enjoyment of freedom which is required
by the fundamental principle of justice. Nor does Kant ever explain
exactly why personal subordinates of citizens cannot enjoy equal political
rights with their superiors; like most of his non-philosophical contemporaries he simply takes it for granted.

The state comprises three authorities, legislative, executive, and
judiciary, each of which has absolute power in its own sphere. The
sovereign legislator enacts positive laws, but cannot be the ruler who
enforces them, for the ruler must be subject to the laws; for the same
reason, although the legislator may depose the ruler, he cannot punish
him, for the right of punishment belongs to the executive power alone.
One might have thought that Kant's insistence on freedom as the fundamental principle of justice would lead him to a liberal view of the relation between subjects and the political authority to which they are
subjected; and so indeed, in theory, it does. He believes that titles of
hereditary nobility should be abolished, for they do not represent any
grading of genuine merit, and he believes that the republican form of
constitution is ultimately the only just one, meaning by 'republican' a
constitution in which the people are in the protection of the people—

D

i.e. in which the people, through its representatives or deputies, is the sovereign legislating body. But where reality falls short of this republican ideal, as it does in almost, if not quite, all existing states, no forcible over-throw of non-republican power, however tyrannically that power is exercised, is permissible. Kant sympathized strongly with the moral principles which he thought were embodied in the French Revolution, or at least in those aspects of it which were opposed to arbitrary and tyrannical government, but he disapproved strongly of its violent methods. He even goes so far as to say that the origin of the supreme political authority is not open to scrutiny by those over whom it is exercised. His argument for this apparently illiberal thesis is curiously abstract: 'In order for the people to be able to judge the supreme political authority with the force of law, it must already be viewed as united under a general legislative will (*Wille*); hence it can and may not judge other-wise than the present chief of state wills' (MdS vi 318). If it were not for the legislative authority, the people would not be a people; hence it can-not legitimately challenge that authority. Illegal resistance to legislation destroys the whole political and legal constitution; for there would be a self-contradiction in any attempt to provide for the right to such resis-tance in the constitution. But from the fact that it would be self-contra-dictory for a constitution to permit unconstitutional resistance to it, Kant's conclusion to the inevitable wrongness of rebellion does not follow. If authority is being exercised with great iniquity and harshness, it is not clear why the ruler should be supposed to possess moral authority at all, nor to possess legal authority except in the obvious sense of authority under his own laws; and why should the subject obey these? In an appendix to the *Metaphysic of Morals* Kant replied to objections of this kind which had appeared in a review of the work; but his reply does not add much to the argument. He says that if a people (*ein Volk*) holds that it is justified in rebelling against a sovereign, this implies that it has a right to make violence instead of justice the supreme principle of law. But it might be retorted that the violence is intended as a once-for-all expedient, not as a principle, and that it is justified, or at least excused, if the activities of the sovereign have led to so much injustice and inter-ference with personal liberty that the fundamental purpose of the state is no longer being fulfilled. No doubt revolution is justified only in extreme circumstances; but Kant's passionate insistence that it is never justified is difficult to square with his equally sincere and genuine devotion to liberty and republicanism and, as with some of the other views expressed in the *Metaphysic of Morals*, it seems more a matter of personal emotion and commitment than the a priori truth of reason which it is supposed to be.[1]

Kant's views on punishment are worth noting. Legal punishment may be imposed only because the man to be punished has committed a crime; but it is a duty of the state to punish crime, not merely a right. Any departure from this strictly retributive approach is an injustice and a transgression of the rights of humanity. The rule which determines the nature and amount of punishment suitable for a particular crime is the principle of equality: if a man has inflicted undeserved harm on another, he must have a similar amount of deserved harm inflicted on him in turn, to redress the balance. Kant thus provides not merely a retributivist justification of punishment, but also a retributivist criterion for the form and degree in which it is to be inflicted. Murder requires the death penalty; there is no other punishment that could in any way equal, and thus be suited to, the crime.

> Even if a civil society were to dissolve itself by common agreement of all its members . . . the last murderer remaining in prison must first be executed, so that everyone will duly receive what his actions are worth and so that the blood-guilt thereof will not be fixed on the people because they failed to insist on carrying out the punishment; for if they fail to do so, they may be regarded as accomplices in this public violation of legal justice. (MdS VI 333.)

It is not altogether clear what this notion of blood-guilt has to do with an a priori rational principle of justice—it seems to have more in common with superstition, a phenomenon against which Kant elsewhere makes strong and effective attacks. It might be that in such a situation it would be wrong to let a murderer loose if he was dangerous and likely to commit more murders, but this is not Kant's argument. He seems to pass too readily in discussions of punishment and desert from the relatively uncontroversial and plausible thesis that a man who has committed a crime may legitimately be punished to the more contentious, not to say dubious, thesis that such a man must be punished (even the sovereign's right of pardon is limited by Kant to the pardoning of crimes against himself); and again, he passes from the plausible thesis that a man may not be punished more severely for a crime than the nature of the crime warrants to the less plausible thesis that a man must receive punishment proportionate to the crime. For Kant, excessive punishment is, of course, an injustice, but it seems to be no worse an injustice than insufficient punishment or no punishment at all.

[1] It is hard to believe that Kant would have regarded Hitler as in any way representing a law and justice which it was an outrageous crime to resist.

Kant's discussion of international law is brief and of no particular philosophical importance. What is important in this context is the way in which he argues for international co-operation and peace, not on simple humanitarian grounds, but as a corollary of the general principles of justice which he has already established. Just as individual men are morally bound to pass out of a state of nature, in which conflict is possible, into a state of civil society, in which it is ruled out, so nations have a duty to pass out of their state of nature, in which war between them is possible, into some relationship analogous to that which joins individuals in civil society; thus and only thus can peace be permanently established. However impracticable union between states and the consequent perpetual peace may be, they are an ideal of justice which men must try to achieve as nearly as possible. In a separate essay entitled *Perpetual Peace*, which was published in 1795, Kant had already indicated some of the steps which needed to be taken towards this end, including, first, provisional articles of agreement and, then, the definitive articles; they are interesting as anticipations of such later developments as the covenant of the League of Nations and the United Nations charter. The three definitive articles are (i) the civil constitution of every state should be republican (not only because republics are preferable in themselves, but also because they are less likely to go to war than despotic states), (ii) the law of nations is to be founded on a federation of free states (since the success of such a federation would make war between its members impossible), and (iii) the law of world citizenship is to be limited to conditions of universal hospitality (the world citizen is to have the right not to be treated as an enemy when he is in a country not his own, but he does not have the right to be treated generously or benevolently, for it is a principle of justice that is in question, not a matter of philanthropy). 'As a matter of fact', Kant concludes, 'it can be said that the establishment of a universal and enduring peace is not just a part, but rather constitutes the whole, of the ultimate purpose of law within the bounds of pure reason' (MdS VI 355).

In order to complete this account of Kant's practical philosophy, we need to consider his view of the relation between morality and religion, and, in particular, his answer to the question how far and in what sense the requirements of morality may be regarded as the commands of God. He discusses this topic principally in his essay *Religion within the Bounds of Reason Alone* (Part I was published in 1792, and the remaining three parts in the following year). The key to his treatment of the subject lies in his thesis that autonomy of the will is the fundamental principle of morality, together with his refutation of the theoretical claims of rational theology. The moral law, as we have seen, commands unconditionally; it says simply 'You must do this' or 'You must not do that', not 'You must do this if you want to achieve that'. Morality, then, does not lay down rules for the service of any interest, whether one's own or another's; it is not reducible to the fulfilment of the desires or commands of anyone—neither one's own desires or inclinations nor the desires or commands of an earthly or supernatural superior. The moral law can preserve its unconditioned character only if it is thought of as springing from the rational will of the very being on whom it is binding; a man is morally subject only to laws which as a rational being he has discovered and imposed on himself.[1]

The refutation of the claims of rational theology renders most of the popular philosophical attempts to connect theology and morality quite pointless. Locke had argued that it should be possible to provide a logical demonstration of moral truths, beginning with a proof of the existence of a supreme being possessing certain clearly defined attributes, and deducing from this the kind of conduct which such a being must will and command us to perform; and many attempts at demonstrations of this kind were made by eighteenth-century writers. But whatever the connexion may be between the will of God and our moral duties, if philosophy cannot demonstrate the existence of God (and, a fortiori, cannot demonstrate that there is a God who requires us to act in certain ways), a philosophical deduction of morality from theology becomes pointless; if we can have no knowledge of the theological premisses—as Kant insists we cannot—then even if we could deduce moral conclusions from them the result would be unhelpful. The fact that Kant himself produces arguments of a sort for the existence of God is beside the point; for these arguments presuppose morality, and cannot therefore be used to justify it.

It has often been held that morality is in some way incomplete without belief in God. The arguments for this view may take a number of different forms, but most of them fall under one of two classes. It may be maintained that there is something logically unsatisfactory about an assertion that one has a moral duty to act in certain ways rather than others unless the assertion can be supported by reference to the command or will of a supreme being: do not such assertions lack something needed in the way

---

[1] A corollary of this is that man needs no incentive to obey the moral law other than pure respect for the law itself; he can, and must, obey it irrespective of any consideration of his own pleasure or profit, or of the pleasure or profit of any other being.

of support or justification, and can this need be fulfilled otherwise than by their being grounded in the will of God? How in the end can we know that we ought to act in certain ways unless we are sure that God, the supreme creator and governor of the universe, requires us so to act? Alternatively, and sometimes simultaneously, it is said that there is no rational motive for doing one's duty when it is more pleasant or advantageous to neglect it unless we suppose that virtue will eventually be rewarded and vice punished, in another world if not in this. Both kinds of argument are clearly inconsistent with the principle of autonomy, and so with the whole concept of morality as Kant understands it.

So far as morality is based upon the conception of man as a free agent who, just because he is free, binds himself through his reason to unconditioned laws, it stands in need neither of the idea of another Being over him, for him to apprehend his duty, nor of an incentive other than the law itself, for him to do his duty. (*Religion* VI 3, tr. p. 3.)

The belief that there is no incentive for a man to do his duty once the threat of divine punishment and the promise of divine reward are removed can be quickly rejected. No doubt there are people who refrain from misbehaving only because of such threats and promises; but their conduct is only outwardly in accordance with the moral law and, since its motive is not respect for the moral law itself, it is no proper object of human admiration or approval nor, for the same reason, will God think it worthy of reward. If we believe that God rewards the virtuous, we cannot think that He makes no distinction between those who are genuinely virtuous, doing their duty for duty's sake, and those who are led to perform externally correct acts for purely self-centred reasons. It is important, Kant holds, not to misunderstand biblical talk of rewards. 'When the Teacher of the Gospel spoke of rewards in the world to come he wished to make them thereby not an incentive to action but merely . . . an object of the purest respect and of the greatest moral approval when reason reviews human destiny in its entirety' (*Religion* VI 162, tr. p. 150). A system of divine government in which happiness is in the end enjoyed in proportion as it has been deserved by morally good conduct is indeed more rational than one in which its distribution is haphazard; but the happiness is deserved only to the extent that the thought of it was not part of the motive to action.

The more important, however, of the views which Kant is opposing is that morality needs a theological foundation before its claims can be regarded as rationally binding. The falsity of the view follows, of course, from Kant's thesis of the autonomy of the will as the fundamental principle of morality. If the moral law is a universal law of reason imposed by a man's will on himself, and if man's capacity for obeying such a law is his only means of escaping the universal causality of the physical world, with its consequent exclusion of the free will necessary for morality, then the knowledge that God requires me to obey the moral law, though it may be emotionally effective, cannot make it more rational and more necessary for me to obey it than it was before.

Suppose then that the theological moralist tries to evade the force of this argument by denying the thesis of autonomy. Those who take this anti-Kantian position and hold that our duties are derived solely from the will or command of God may legitimately be asked whether any notion of goodness, analogous to, though not necessarily identical with, moral goodness is included in their conception of God. If it is not, and if God's will is supposed to be binding on us merely because of his omnipotence and omniscience, then, Kant argues, we are being asked to accept superstition, not religion. Mere power, apart from authority, can create no moral obligation at all. It is no defence against this objection to say that God cannot be the subject of moral attributes in precisely the same way as human beings—that God, though good in a sense, is good in a different sense. The difference, though it exists for Kant, does not affect the argument, for it consists merely in the fact that God has no inclinations or appetites which might lead him to will or act in a way contrary to reason, and that for Him therefore, unlike men, the moral law does not take the form of enjoining a duty which he must perform whether he wants to or not; the notions of duty and obligation do not apply to God, who has a holy will which inevitably wills what is good. But the principle of goodness is essentially the same for the divine as for the human will: for God, as for man, the good will is the rational will.

Suppose, then, that we assert that God is necessarily good and that this is a synthetic, not an analytic, proposition (i.e. 'good' is not defined, as it is by nominalists such as William of Ockham, as 'that which God wills'); cannot this notion of God function as a foundation of morality? Kant's reply is that any assertion that God, so understood, requires or commands us to act in certain ways needs itself to be tested by the rules of morality; in other words, morality is still the logical starting-point. 'Even though something is represented as commanded by God, through a direct manifestation of Him, yet, if it flatly contradicts morality, it cannot, despite all appearances, be of God (e.g. were a father ordered to kill his son who is, so far as he knows, perfectly innocent)' (*Religion* VI 87, tr. pp. 81–82).

The whole of revealed religion, including the Bible, needs to be interpreted with the requirements of morality firmly in mind; we must always
prefer a moral interpretation to a literal one, if the latter has immoral
implications. If we find, for example, as we are liable to find, especially
in the Old Testament, stories which apparently allow or even approve of
actions of personal revenge, we must either interpret them in such a way
as to remove all reference to such approval (allegorically or symbolically,
perhaps) or else we must say that the stories cannot represent the will of
God, and that this part of the Bible cannot be as divinely inspired as the
Church maintains it to be. Again, the inquisitor who thinks that God
requires him to condemn a heretic to be burnt at the stake is at fault, even
though he appears to do what he believes to be right; he should argue
that the ill treatment of the morally innocent is morally wrong and that
therefore God cannot want or require him to do it, whatever his eccle-
siastical superiors or his own interpretation of the Bible may suggest to
the contrary.

There is indeed, for Kant, no authoritative source of knowledge of
God's will outside the moral judgement of the individual man, who must
judge all purported revelations of God's commands in the light of the
moral ideals prescribed to him by his own reason. His reason is able to tell
him that, just as it is wrong for him to inflict undeserved suffering on
another man, so, and for exactly the same reasons, it would be wrong
for an all-powerful supernatural being to inflict undeserved suffering on
men, and thus impossible for God, who is supremely rational and
good, to do so.

Though it does indeed sound dangerous, it is in no way reprehensible to say
that every man *creates a God* for himself, nay, must make himself such a God
according to moral concepts. . . . For in whatever manner a being has been made
known to him by another and described as God, yea, even if such a being had
appeared to him (if this is possible), he must first of all compare this representation with his ideal in order to judge whether he is entitled to regard it and to
honour it as a divinity. (*Religion* VI 168 n., tr. p. 157 n.)

Many erroneous views on this topic are fostered, Kant thinks, by faults
in the upbringing of children; the ideal method of inculcating sound
moral and religious ideas in the young, he suggests in his lectures on
Education, although it is in the present state of society a practical impossibility, would be to prevent a child from hearing the word 'God' and
learning the concept of a powerful creator and governor of the universe
until he had first received a thorough moral training; the moral principles
could then be safely transferred to the notion of the divine being. As

things are, however, children are taught to fear God's power rather than reverence his goodness, and fear rather than a genuine sense of duty becomes the motive of many of their dutiful actions. It is in any case far easier for a child to learn that an action is unjust or wrong than to learn and understand the concept of a supreme being. A little later on in the same lectures, Kant makes a more general attack on attempts to establish religion independently of moral considerations:

Religion without moral conscientiousness is a service of superstition. People want to serve God by praising Him and reverencing His power and wisdom, without thinking how to fulfil the divine law; nay, even without knowing and searching out His power, wisdom, etc. These hymn-singings are an opiate for the conscience of such people, and a pillow on which it may quietly slumber. (IX 495.)

Kant is sometimes criticized for passing uncritically from the thesis that morality is necessary to religion to the less plausible thesis that morality is sufficient; and his fondness for such remarks as 'Religion is morality applied to the knowledge of God' (*Lectures on Education* IX 494) and 'Religion is the recognition of all duties as divine commands' (KPV V 129) might lend some support to this criticism. When Kant is emphasizing the moral content of religion he is inclined to give the impression that he regards God's only function as that of emphasizing the moral law and creating and preserving conditions in which those who obey it may in the end hope for happiness in proportion as they have deserved it. It is true also that he has no use for such Christian concepts as grace, salvation, and the service of God except in so far as they are given a moral interpretation: the service of God consists in leading a morally good life, not in rites and observances, and grace and salvation are earned by moral goodness and nothing else—Kant will have no truck with the doctrine of justification by faith. But although he does exclude from his concept of religion, and especially from that of the Christian religion, of which he regards himself as an adherent, much that is commonly held to belong to it, he is not as narrowly moralistic about it as some of his less cautious remarks, taken out of context, might suggest. The religious emotions of wonder and awe are not limited by him to moral objects, but are directed also to the vast spaces of the physical world; to recall the famous passage at the end of the *Critique of Practical Reason*, 'Two things fill the mind with ever new and increasing admiration and awe, the oftener and more steadily they are reflected on: the starry heavens above me and the moral law within me' (KPV V 161). Kant has great feeling for the sublimity of nature and does not deny that a feeling of this kind can be essentially religious in form, provided that it is joined to a respect for God's moral holiness; when this respect is absent, however, religion degenerates into superstition, and our attitude becomes simply one of dread for the powerful and dangerous forces of a nature which we do not understand and which we cannot control. Considered as mere animals we are indeed insignificant before the vastness of the physical universe; considered as men—i.e. as rational, and therefore moral, beings—we are its superiors, and the superiors of any display of mere power and might.

The man that is actually in a state of fear, finding in himself good reason to be so, because he is conscious of offending with his evil disposition against a might directed by a will at once irresistible and just, is far from being in the frame of mind for admiring divine greatness, for which a temper of calm reflection and a quite free judgement are required. Only when he becomes conscious of having a disposition that is upright and acceptable to God, do those operations of might serve to stir within him the idea of the sublimity of this Being, so far as he recognizes the existence in himself of a sublimity of disposition consonant with His will, and is thus raised above the dread of such operations of nature, in which he no longer sees God pouring forth the vials of his wrath. (KU v 263.)

# 4
# Aesthetics and Teleology

THE READER OF THE FIRST TWO *Critiques* might be pardoned for wondering what room there was for a third. Reason works theoretically and practically; the *Critique of Pure Reason*, in spite of its more general title, was devoted principally to an analysis of the theoretical activities of reason and their limitations, and the *Critique of Practical Reason* had a corresponding function in respect of practical thinking. Between them, do they not fulfil Kant's original intention of investigating critically and analytically the human mind and its capacity for knowledge? It seems clear that, although Kant had often thought of writing what he called a critique of taste, in which beauty and related notions would be discussed, he had had no idea when working on the first *Critique* that this would form part of a third major work in the critical series,[1] and no idea that our power of judging would require so extended a discussion. Judgement is discussed briefly in the *Critique of Pure Reason* and its treatment there is quite straightforward. 'If understanding in general is to be viewed as the faculty of rules, judgement will be the faculty of subsuming under rules; that is, of distinguishing whether something does or does not stand under a given rule (*casus datae legis*)' (KRV A132 B171). Concepts are rules; the subsumption of particulars under concepts is either empirical ('this is a dog') or a priori ('this is a triangle', 'that is a substance') and, in either case, the rules are supplied by the understanding, or by the understanding and sensibility combined. There are no rules for making judgements and at this level, therefore, there is no need for a critical examination of the faculty of judging over and above the critical examination of the understanding that is contained in the *Critique of Pure Reason*.

[1] During his critical period, Kant's plans for writing continually changed, and his announced plans were rarely adhered to. Some information about his intentions can be gathered from letters which he wrote from time to time to such friends as Garve and Reinhold, but the exact course of events is difficult, if not impossible, to trace with certainty.

But the activity of judging, Kant points out in the *Critique of Judgement*, is not limited to this straightforward one of thinking that a particular object given in intuition falls under a given, known concept.

The judgement can be regarded either as a mere capacity for *reflecting* on a given representation according to a certain 'principle, to produce a possible concept, or as a capacity for *making determinate* a basic concept by means of a given empirical representation. In the first case it is the *reflective*, in the second the *determining* judgement. To *reflect* (or to deliberate) is to compare and combine given representations either with other representations or with one's cognitive powers, with respect to a concept which is thereby made possible. (KU First Introduction XX 211.)[1]

What Kant now calls determining judgement is as straightforward as he seems to have thought judgement as a whole to be, when he wrote the first *Critique*: its function is to apply universal concepts of the understanding to particulars given in intuition. Reflective judgement, we now learn, is concerned not with the categories or concepts of the understanding which are the necessary conditions of experience in general, but with empirical concepts and with the necessary conditions of their formation. Our ability to judge that an individual empirical object given us in intuition falls under an empirical concept has transcendental implications, and it is the purpose of the *Critique of Judgement* to establish these implications. We can, if we like, express the difference by speaking of laws rather than concepts: the deduction and the schematism of the categories referred to the universal laws of thought in general (which are, of course, applicable both to ordinary and to scientific thinking); the reflective judgement, on the other hand, is concerned with empirical laws of nature—it takes a given phenomenon and asks 'Under what more general law or concept is this phenomenon to be subsumed?'

Our higher capacity for thought has three aspects, understanding, which is the ability to have knowledge of the universal, judgement, which is the capacity for subsuming the particular under the universal, and reason, which is the capacity for determining the particular through the universal (for making deductions from principles). The understanding furnishes a priori laws of nature, and reason furnishes a priori laws of freedom—so much has been demonstrated in the first and second *Critiques* respectively. We may therefore expect judgement to furnish a priori principles of its own. Yet judgement is not an independent cognitive capacity; it does not provide us with concepts (like understanding)

---

[1] This First Introduction was omitted by Kant from the published *Critique* because of its excessive length; but it forms an invaluable guide to the main principles of the work.

or Ideas (like reason). 'Therefore, should there be a concept or rule which has sprung originally from the faculty of judgement, it would have to be a concept of things *in nature so far as nature conforms to our power of judgement*' (KU First Introduction XX 202). In discussing natural phenomena and the system to which they belong we can say that, in order to be able to know nature, 'we must be able to judge the particular to be contained under the universal and to subsume it under the concept of nature as one' (ibid. 202-3). A certain simplicity is required in nature if our faculty of judgement is not to find its work impossible; there might conceivably be such a multiplicity of empirical laws and so great a heterogeneity of natural forms that we could not reduce them to any kind of system, and this would mean that we could have no scientific knowledge of nature at all. Natural science requires us to be able to judge that this object belongs to a certain species, and that this is in its turn a species of a certain genus; and judging of this kind would be impossible if nature were not in a sense adapted to our powers of judging. This adaptation of nature to our mental faculties is not an objective principle—we have no direct knowledge that nature is, in itself, adapted in this purposive way—but a subjective principle which we have to use in order to direct our inquiries into nature. In technical terms, the principle belongs to reflective, not to determinant, judgement and is a regulative, not a constitutive principle of reason, in the wide sense of this last word. We have to regard nature as if it were the product of art.[1]

The distinction between understanding, reason, and judgement is connected with another threefold distinction. All the powers of the human mind reduce in the end to three: (i) the cognitive faculty (*das Erkenntnisvermögen*), (ii) the faculty of desire (or the appetitive faculty—*das Begehrungsvermögen*), and (iii) the feeling of pleasure and displeasure (*das Gefühl der Lust und Unlust*). The first of these is concerned with knowledge of an object, the second with the determination to bring an object into existence, and the third with the feeling of pleasure or displeasure at the existence of an object. Some pleasure is, of course, dependent on the satisfaction of desire; and when this happens, (iii) is subordinate to (ii). But this is not true of all pleasure, some of which is

---

[1] It is not that we discover empirically that nature is simple. The most we could discover empirically would be that those parts of nature which we had so far investigated were simple; and this would still leave open the possibility that some parts of it are complicated. Kant's point is rather that the simplicity of nature is presupposed by our ability to have any sort of natural science at all; we know a priori that nature must be like this if we are to have any systematic empirical knowledge of it.

independent of desire and thus requires independent critical treatment. Now our ability to obtain knowledge through concepts has its a priori principle in the pure understanding, and our ability to set ourselves to bring about desired ends has its a priori principle in pure reason. We might therefore expect the feeling of pleasure and displeasure to find *its* a priori principle in the faculty of judgement; and this, in Kant's view, is what we do find. The reason for this link seems to lie in their common subjectivity. Judgement, unlike reason and understanding, is always relative to the judging subject; and the feeling of pleasure and displeasure, unlike the cognitive and appetitive faculties, is merely sensitivity to a state of the subject—'so that if the judgement is always to determine something for itself alone, this probably could be only the feeling of pleasure; and conversely if the latter is always to have a principle a priori, it will only be found in the judgement' (KU First Introduction xx 208).

There are two ways in which we may regard the purposiveness of natural forms, one aesthetic, the other teleological. Putting it for the moment in a misleadingly simple way, we may judge things in nature to be so constructed as to harmonize with our mental faculties, especially those of imagination and understanding, thus causing us a special kind of disinterested pleasure; or we may judge them to be so constructed as to fulfil certain purposes in nature. We may judge of a woman, for example, that she has beautiful eyes, and we may also judge that her eyes were given her to see with; and both these judgements may give rise to pleasure, since we derive disinterested pleasure also from seeing the ways in which objects and phenomena seem to work together for an end or ends. We must not suppose that either kind of purposiveness is actually intended or designed. We are viewing nature as if it were a work of art, but not saying that it is actually and objectively one; the judgement of purposiveness is reflective, not determinant, as it is when we say that some lines of a drawing have a certain function or purpose relative to the work as a whole.

It was pointed out in the first *Critique* that there are four logical functions of judgement, Quality, Quantity, Relation, and Modality (cf. KRV A70). The part of the *Critique of Judgement* which treats of aesthetics begins by enunciating four propositions about beauty, each of which corresponds to one of these functions or moments. In terms of the logical quality of an aesthetic judgement, we obtain this: '*Taste* is the faculty of judging an object or a mode of representing it by a *wholly disinterested* pleasure or displeasure. The object of such pleasure is called *beautiful*' (KU v 211, tr. p. 12). Suppose we observe a well-proportioned and well-designed building, and derive a feeling of well-being or a sense of heightened vitality from contemplating it; our judgement that the building is beautiful will be based on the fact that it gives rise to a sensuous feeling of pleasure, i.e. it will be a subjective judgement. But it is not just any pleasure that justifies us in saying that its cause or object is beautiful. We frequently take pleasure in the existence of an object because we think of it as being useful or good, and this pleasure has nothing to do with a judgement of taste. We must distinguish the aesthetic pleasure which we receive from contemplating a visually attractive new hospital, for example, from the pleasure which we may take in the thought of the contribution which the hospital may make to public welfare. Judgements which attribute usefulness or absolute, that is moral, goodness to the existence of an object have their roots in the appetitive faculty, and appeal to desire or will. But the judgement of taste has nothing to do with desire; it is purely contemplative. Pleasure in the beautiful is disinterested and therefore free, and is the only pleasure of this kind.

Under the heading of logical quantity, the beautiful is characterized thus: 'That in which we take a pleasure that is universal and yet independent of concepts is beautiful' (KU v 219, tr. p. 23). The stress here is on the universality of the pleasure which is aroused by the contemplation of what is beautiful, and the universality is said by Kant to follow from its disinterestedness. A man who judges that an object is beautiful indicates that his judgement does not depend for its truth on any personal inclination or on any private condition which affects him alone; 'he must therefore regard his pleasure as grounded on what he may also presuppose in everyone else' (KU v 211, tr. p. 13). But although aesthetic judgements are universal, their universality is subjective, not objective, as is that of so-called logical judgements (i.e. judgements which are based on concepts). When we judge that something we see is a rose, we are judging in accordance with a rule, that is, in accordance with the concept rose; our judgement is true or false according as its subject does or does not objectively fall under the concept. When we judge that something we see is beautiful, however, we are not judging in accordance with a rule; for, Kant holds, there are no rules, reasons, or principles by means of which it can be proved that a particular object is beautiful. What happens is that we assume or presuppose universal agreement with our judgement, as if it were one which subsumed a case under a rule; and we are right to make this presupposition, provided that we have abstracted from our judgement everything that belongs only to the class of the merely pleasant, the useful, or the morally good.

The contrast between the beautiful and the merely pleasant is important here. According to Kant, the judgement that this wine has a pleasant taste is purely subjective and has no universal reference; the man who makes it must admit that he can legitimately mean no more by it than that the wine tastes pleasant to him. It is in this context, not in that of the aesthetic judgement of beauty, that the proverb 'Everyone has his own taste' is true. There is no contradiction between 'This wine tastes pleasant (sc. to me)' said by one man and 'This wine tastes unpleasant (sc. to me)' said by another; but if one man says of a building 'That is beautiful' and another says of the same building 'That is not beautiful', they are contradicting one another, and cannot both be right. When we say that something is beautiful we demand agreement from others and object to disagreement; we can distinguish good from bad taste.

Now since the judgement that a thing is beautiful is always accompanied by pleasure, the question arises, Which comes first, the judgement or the pleasure? The solution of this problem, Kant says, is the key to the critique of taste. His answer, as we should expect, is that the judgement precedes the pleasure; for otherwise, judgements of beauty would be as subjective and private as judgements of mere pleasantness—they would be merely empirical, depending solely on the fact that a particular sensation happened to give pleasure to a particular individual. But if the judgement of beauty precedes the pleasure, what is there in the judgement that gives rise to the pleasure? Kant's answer to this question is of great importance. We have seen that concepts are not involved in judgements of taste; those of our mental powers which are active in judging that a thing is beautiful and in being aware of the consequent pleasure are not limited in their activity by any particular rule. 'Hence', Kant concludes, 'the mental state in this representation must be one of feeling the free play of the powers of representation, namely, such a free play at the occasion of a given representation as is generally suitable for a cognition' (KU v 217, tr. p. 21). In particular, the pleasure consists in the free play given to the powers of imagination and reason in the contemplation of the beautiful object. What Kant means by this rather obscure general statement seems to be something like this. When I contemplate a rose, judge that it is beautiful, and take pleasure in its beauty, the source of my pleasure is not the existence of the rose, but a kind of harmony which exists between the two relevant faculties of my mind, my imagination (by which is meant here simply my power of forming images), and my intellect (which unites the images into a unified whole). The rose is judged beautiful as being fitted to occasion or express this mental harmony. The universality of aesthetic judgements is thus derivable from the fact that the essential structure of the human mind does not differ as between one man and another; if any object gives rise to this pleasurable feeling of harmony in one man, we are entitled to assume that it is capable of doing the same for any other.

A representation, though single and apart from any comparison with others, may yet be tuned to the conditions of universality, which constitutes the general business of reason. It then brings the cognitive faculties into that proportionate harmony which is required for all cognition and therefore deemed valid for everyone whose characteristic it is to judge by a co-operation of reason and senses (that is, for every human being). (KU v 219, tr. p. 23.)

The logical function of relation gives us a third proposition about beauty: '*Beauty* is the form of *purposiveness* in an object so far as this form is perceived in it *without the concept of a purpose*' (KU v 236, tr. p. 45). We come across many objects which have come into being as the result of a conscious decision on the part of some agent to produce them; a watch, for example, has the structure it has, and the component parts have the various functions they have, because this structure and these functions have been intentionally and designedly built into the watch by its maker. In such cases we may apply the word 'purposive' either to the designed object, or to the action or state of mind of the designer or maker. It is in a rather different way that the notion of purposiveness enters into Kant's account of beauty. There are, he says, objects or states of mind or actions which may be called purposive in a sense, even though we do not, by so calling them, imply that they are the result of conscious purpose or design on the part of any being. This 'purposiveness without purpose' (*Zweckmässigkeit ohne Zweck*) exists when, although we do not assert or imply an actual conscious purpose, we find that we cannot understand the possibility of a form or structure except by regarding it as if it sprang from a will (it will appear from the teleological section of the *Critique* that all living things are purposive in this sense; here, however, we are concerned only with the 'purposiveness' of beautiful objects).

With artifacts in general, that is with objects which have been designed with a purpose in view, we tend to derive pleasure from their contemplation, Kant thinks, to the extent that they satisfactorily fulfil, and continue to fulfil, the purpose or purposes of their designer or maker. Pleasure of this kind, however, is irrelevant to judgements of taste; if we take pleasure in the satisfactory working of the parts of a watch, it is because this satisfactory working has a practical value and contributes to some human interest—and Kant has already argued that a judgement that an object is beautiful cannot be based on any interest or value of this kind. 'The judgement of taste', as he puts it somewhat obscurely, 'has to do exclusively with the relation of the representational faculties to one another so far as this relation is determined by a representation' (KU V 221, tr. p. 25). What Kant means is this. The purposiveness which we seem to find in a beautiful object is not actually in the object itself, for we have no means of knowing whether natural beauty is the product of design; it is rather the result of the activity of our own contemplating mind, and it is this activity which supplies the element of purposiveness. We do not judge an object as beautiful because we think of it as having been consciously and effectively designed; we judge it as beautiful because, in order to understand its effect, we have to think of it as if it had been so designed. It is beautiful because, if it had been designed, it would have been well designed; well designed, that is, to appeal to, and cause pleasure to, our contemplating mind. Indeed, in Kant's view, what we are really taking pleasure in when we feel pleasure as the result of judging something to be beautiful is not anything in the beautiful object itself, but rather the activity or free play of our own cognitive powers. Contemplation of the beautiful is thus self-perpetuating; 'we *dwell* upon the contemplation of the beautiful because this contemplation strengthens and reproduces itself' (KU V 222, tr. 27). The judgement that an object is beautiful is based on a felt harmony in the play of our mental powers when they contemplate that object.

Kant insists that judgements of taste concern, strictly speaking, only the appreciation of formal elements in the beautiful objects; sensuous and emotional factors must both be excluded. If a statue has been painted in a bright colour in order that it may have an added superficial attractiveness, this colour cannot contribute in any way to its beauty, strictly and properly so called. On the other hand, the way in which colour is used in a painting can contribute to its beauty to the extent that it is considered as part of the painting's formal structure.

If the purity of colours and tones, or their variety and contrast, seem to contribute to beauty, this must not be misunderstood to mean that they supply, as it were, a homogeneous addition to the pleasure in the form because they are pleasant themselves. It does mean that they render the perception of the form more precise, more definite, and more complete. (KU V 225-6, tr. p. 31.)

Emotional appeal, similarly, is not a constituent of beauty (sublimity, however, which is an important aesthetic feature of many works of art, as well as of natural scenes and objects, is bound up with emotion, as we shall see later).

Kant proceeds to make a distinction which further emphasizes the need to distinguish pure judgements of aesthetic taste from judgements which, though they are connected in some ways with judgements of taste or have some resemblance to them, are themselves relatively impure. This is the distinction between free and dependent beauty. We may on occasion judge a building (a church, for example) to be beautiful partly, at least, because we have an idea of what a church ought to be; the beauty is here dependent on our concept of a church, and is thus not part of a free and pure judgement of taste, since its dependence on the concept restricts the free play of our imagination—our contemplation of the church is confined within limits by reflection on the nature and function of churches.[1] Free beauty, on the other hand, exists where there are no such normative ideas or concepts; flower-blossoms, birds of paradise, many kinds of sea-shell, non-figurative drawings such as designs on wallpapers, and music which is not a setting of words are given by Kant as examples (even though a botanist may have some idea of what sort of thing a flower ought to be, he does not take this notion of natural purpose into account when judging its beauty). Some of the disagreements which occur over the question whether a given object is beautiful are caused, Kant thinks, by a failure to distinguish these two types of beauty; one man may think a palace beautiful, another not, because the first judges it as a case of free beauty, whereas the other, though he might acknowledge the formal perfection of its design, nevertheless thinks that it does not look the way a palace ought to look, and is therefore lacking in dependent beauty.

The fourth, and last, logical aspect of judgement gives us '*Beautiful* is that which is recognized without concepts to be the object of a *necessary* pleasure' (KU v 240, tr. p. 51). The emphasis here is on the necessity of the pleasure which we take in what is beautiful. Up to now we have come across two main types of philosophical necessity in Kant's critical philosophy. First, there is the theoretical, objective necessity that belongs to a priori cognitive judgements (for example, the necessity which is involved in the proposition, known by us to be true, that every event has as its cause, or ground, some other event preceding it in time). Secondly,

---

[1] Dependent beauty does not belong to artifacts alone, but to human beings, animals, and plants as well.

there is the practical necessity which is bound up with morality (the necessity to act in a certain way). Both these types of necessity are unconditioned. Now necessity of some kind must belong to aesthetic judgements; it is not a brute, contingent fact that some shapes or sounds cause us aesthetic pleasure and others do not. But it cannot be an objective necessity of either the theoretical or the practical type; we do not know that everyone does or will find pleasure in an object which we rightly assert to be beautiful. The judgement of taste, in Kant's view, hopes for, or expects (the verb is *ansinnen*), even though it does not strictly and logically demand, universal assent; if someone fails to find beautiful something that I do think beautiful, then although I do not have to suppose that he has made an empirical or a conceptual error, I nevertheless imply that he is failing to make a judgement which a person of proper sensitivity would make. So, Kant concludes, since judgements of taste are based on feeling or sense, they must be based on a common feeling or sense[1] (*Gemeinsinn*), rather than a merely private one; in the latter case they would be indistinguishable from the completely subjective judgements of pleasantness, and would have no necessity whatsoever. This common feeling or sensibility is an ideal norm or standard, the presupposing of which is enough to convert any judgement which agrees with it into a rule which must be accepted by everyone.

Kant summarizes his entire fourfold analysis of the concept of beauty by saying that taste is the faculty of judging an object with respect to the free conformity of the imagination to law. The imagination here works freely and spontaneously, not being tied down to a definite form as it is in judgements of sense-perception. Aesthetic pleasure consists in the exercise and entertainment of our mental faculties in a free and indeterminately purposive way by what we call beautiful; reason is thereby put to the service of imagination.

So far, Kant has been expounding the nature of a judgement that an object is beautiful (in an Analytic, to use his technical term), while taking for granted the legitimacy of such judgements, thus analysed and expounded. But judgements of taste, like all other judgements which lay claim to necessity, need a 'deduction'; that is to say, our right to make them needs to be demonstrated. How are judgements of taste possible, then, and, in particular, how can we justify our expectation or demand that, when we take pleasure in something which we judge to be beautiful, our pleasure should be shared by anyone else who contemplates the

[1] This, of course, has nothing to do with what is ordinarily called 'common sense', the mark of the sensible man as opposed to the stupid one.

same object? This is the *Critique of Judgement*'s special version of the general problem of transcendental philosophy, How are synthetic a priori judgements possible? We have already seen that aesthetic judgements are necessary and a priori; and it is clear that they must be synthetic, for the feeling of pleasure aroused by the contemplation of a beautiful object cannot be part of the concept or intuition of that object.

Before proceeding to answer the question he has posed, Kant makes a number of preliminary remarks. The first of these confirms a point already made, that although judgements of taste are essentially subjective, they do nevertheless behave in some respects as if they were objective; and this quasi-objectivity (exemplified in the fact that my judgement that this flower is beautiful, though it is grounded in the taste of an individual, expects universal assent) can be derived only from the fact that the beautiful object is somehow adapted to our faculty of apprehension. There is an affinity, as it were, not just between the beautiful flower and the mental faculties of one particular observer, but between the flower and the human mental faculties in general, qualities that belong to the human intellect and imagination as such, not to this man's intellect and imagination rather than that.

On the other hand, Kant insists, the judgement of taste is like a completely subjective judgement in this respect, that proofs and arguments are quite unable to establish its truth. That a given object is beautiful cannot be proved empirically; in particular, it cannot be proved by counting the number of those who judge it to be beautiful. Nor can it be proved a priori, by showing that the object conforms to certain rules or canons of taste.[1]

> If anyone reads me his poem, or brings me to a play, which, all said and done, fails to commend itself to my taste, then let him adduce Batteux or Lessing, or still older and more famous critics of taste, with all the host of rules laid down by them, as a proof of the beauty of his poem; let certain passages particularly displeasing to me accord completely with the rules of beauty (as set out by these critics and universally recognized): I stop my ears: I do not want to hear any reasons or any arguing about the matter. I would prefer to suppose that those rules of the critics were at fault, or at least have no application, than to allow my judgement to be determined by *a priori* proofs. I take my stand on the ground that my judgement is to be one of taste, and not one of understanding and reason. (KU v 284.)

It follows that a critical investigation of taste cannot be directed towards the discovery of rules for judging the beauty of nature or art; what it

---

[1] Reliance on rules of this kind was a common feature of eighteenth-century criticism.

can, and must, do, according to Kant, is discover the rules which govern the relation and interaction of the understanding and the imagination in the making of aesthetic judgements—indeed, if it is to form part of the critical philosophy, it must do this from an examination of the nature of these faculties alone. Since the imagination is a faculty which exhibits freedom, while the understanding exhibits conformity to law, the subjective power of judgement that constitutes taste must depend on the possibility of somehow bringing the free imagination and the law-abiding understanding into conformity or consonance with one another. This must be a special kind of conformity, distinct from that which occurs in ordinary empirical judgements. Any empirical judgement, as was made clear in the *Critique of Pure Reason*, involves the bringing together of intuitions (the work of the imagination) and concepts (the work of the understanding); but in such judgements there is no freedom at all, nothing but conformity to law and to definite concepts. 'Only when the imagination in its freedom stirs the understanding, and the understanding apart from concepts puts the imagination into regular play, does the representation communicate itself, not as thought, but as an internal feeling of a purposive state of the mind' (KU v 295-6).

The deduction itself, Kant asserts, is easy once the problem has been stated in these terms; for once it has been made clear that the beauty of an object depends solely on its formal properties and, in particular, on the aptness of those formal properties to give rise to a certain kind of *rapport*, as it were, between imagination and understanding, no more is needed than the certainty that the structure of the human imagination and understanding is not a matter of individual idiosyncrasy, but is a universal fact. And this, Kant holds, is indisputable, since if it were not for this universal identity of structure the communication of images and thoughts would be impossible. We are entitled to expect universality of feeling in judgements of taste (i.e. to expect that others' judgements should agree with ours, provided always that ours *is* a judgement of taste, untainted by irrelevant feelings of non-aesthetic pleasure or by considerations of prudential interest or moral worth) because the very fact that feelings are universally communicable as a result of the essential identity of structure in the human mind creates an interest in what is beautiful. In other words, although the judgement that an object is beautiful is not derived from, and must not be confused with, any interest in or desire for the existence of that object, such an interest or desire can nevertheless arise once the judgement of taste has been made.

Now there is an empirical interest of this general kind, which arises from man's natural propensity to society; sociability leads a man to communicate his aesthetic pleasure to others, and this is why, when constructing useful objects such as boats or clothes, he will take care to see that they are not merely useful but attractively coloured and shaped as well. But this empirical interest concerns only what is superficially charming rather than the profoundly beautiful, and cannot in any case play a part in an a priori deduction or in any aspect of the critique of taste. What is important is the a priori, or intellectual, interest in the beautiful. It is at this point that we discover the justification for Kant's firm belief in the superiority of the beauties of nature over those of art. A man who admires and loves the beautiful form of a wild flower or a bird or some other product of nature may be said to be glad, in an entirely unselfish and disinterested way, that these things exist; he not merely takes pleasure in the formal aspects of the products of nature, he also takes pleasure in the existence of those products just because they have these formal qualities. This is because, entirely apart from any question of personal gain or advantage, man in general, as a rational being, cannot help being pleased by every indication that nature is so constituted as to cause disinterested pleasure to men through the affinity between it, or some of its aspects, and his imaginative and intellectual faculties. There is no comparable second-order pleasure, however, where works of art are concerned; and although we may temporarily feel the same pleasure in the imitation by a human being of, say, the song of a nightingale, the pleasure ceases as soon as we discover it to be an imitation rather than the real thing. As to serious works of art, Kant's point seems to be that, however impressed we may be by them, it is in principle less remarkable that the product of the mental processes of one man should appeal to the minds of other men than that the products of nature (whose origin, whatever it may be, is not human) should have this affinity and appeal. The suggestion is that, if nature has not been created, in part at least, for our aesthetic delight, we may at least regard it as if it had been so created; and this is remarkable, whereas the production by a man of a poem or a symphony for our pleasure is not. We expect to see order and purposiveness in a work of art, as in many other products of human agency; but to discover them in a non-human aspect of the world is far more impressive and wonderful.

Moreover, our interest in the beauties of nature is akin to moral feeling in a way in which the appreciation of works of art is not; a thoroughly bad man may enjoy and appreciate works of art but he will not, in Kant's view, enjoy the beauties of nature. There is in fact a kind of analogy between natural beauty and morality, which is illustrated by our tendency to apply to aesthetic objects terms which belong originally to the assessment of moral character. We speak of buildings or trees as majestic and stately, of plains as laughing or gay; and we think of the white of the lily as symbolizing innocence, and of the song of a bird as expressing content-ment with its existence.

Taste is, in the ultimate analysis, a critical faculty that judges of the rendering of moral ideas in terms of sense (through the intervention of a certain analogy in our reflection on both); and it is this rendering also, and the increased sensibility founded upon it, for the feeling which these ideas evoke (termed moral sense), that are the origin of that pleasure which taste declares valid for mankind in general and not merely for the private feeling of each individual. This makes it clear that the true propaedeutic for laying the foundations of taste is the develop-ment of moral ideas and the cultivation of the moral feeling. For only when sensi-bility is brought into harmony with moral feeling can genuine taste assume a definite unchangeable form. (KU v 356.)

Kant follows the eighteenth-century convention of grouping together the notions of the beautiful and the sublime and regarding them as con-stituting jointly the aesthetic aspect of nature and the essential qualities of fine art. Judgements of sublimity have certain things in common with judgements of beauty. The beautiful and the sublime are both sources of pleasure, and in both cases this pleasure is not a mere matter of sensation, nor is it dependent on a definite concept, as is the pleasure we take in what is morally good or advantageous, but is due to the ability of the beautiful or sublime object to appeal to the affinity between our imagina-tion and our intellect. There are, however, four important differences. First, the beautiful in nature is associated with the notion of form, which must consist in a kind of limitation, whereas the sublime is associated with the thought of an object as unlimited or boundless and, to that extent, as formless. Secondly, the beautiful is associated with a feeling of the furtherance or enhancement of life (*ein Gefühl der Beförderung des Lebens*) and can be charming and playful: the sublime has no charms and, although it is pleasing, the pleasure we take in it is indirect, arising from alternating repulsion and attraction—and the imagination is in earnest, not at play. Thirdly, sublime objects in nature, so far from appearing, as do beautiful objects, as pre-adapted to our powers of judgement, seem to have no corresponding purposive aspect; a sublime object may be judged all the more sublime precisely because we realize that it is too great to be encompassed or understood by our limited imaginative and intellectual powers. It is for this reason that, according to Kant, natural objects are not themselves, strictly speaking, sublime, but rather express and evoke a kind of sublimity in the human mind. Fourthly and finally, natural beauty is connected with notions of law (even though the law is teleological, not physical law), whereas the sublime has no such connexion, ideas of sublimity being often excited by the wilder and more chaotic aspects of nature. In general, the concept of the sublime is therefore less philosophically important than that of beauty, since it gives no indication of the existence of any purposiveness in nature.

The sublime has two divisions, the mathematical and the dynamical. The mathematically sublime is that in nature which possesses absolute greatness, i.e. that in relation to which everything else is small. We judge a phenomenon of nature to be sublime when its intuition conveys an impression of its infinite size. It can impress us as infinite only because of the inadequacy of our own imaginations to comprehend it; and in judging that an object is mathematically sublime we are, in effect, judging that our mental powers are thus inadequate. We can, of course, through the exercise of our cognitive faculties, come to have knowledge of things which we are unable to imagine (the notion of mathematical infinity, for example); and our reflection on natural sublimity can thus lead us to see the superiority of our rational cognitive faculties over sensibility and imagination. Indeed, the pleasure which we derive from this kind of sublimity is essentially pleasure in our discovery that all standards of sensibility fall short of ideas of reason.

The feeling of the sublime is, therefore, at once a feeling of displeasure, arising from the inadequacy of imagination in the aesthetic estimation of magnitude to attain to its estimation by reason, and a simultaneously awakened pleasure, arising from this very judgement of the inadequacy of the greatest faculty of sense being in accord with ideas of reason, so far as the effort to attain to these is for us a law. It is, in other words, for us a law (of reason), which goes to make us what we are, that we should esteem as small in comparison with ideas of reason everything which for us is great in nature as an object of sense; and that which makes us alive to the feeling of this supersensible side of our being harmonises with that law. (KU v 257.)

The dynamically sublime, as its name suggests, concerns the power of natural objects rather than their size. To regard a natural phenomenon as dynamically sublime is to regard it as fearful (i.e. as something of which it is natural to be afraid) without actually being afraid of it. The eruption of a volcano or the force of a hurricane may be the source of an aesthetic pleasure in the sublime when we view them from a place of safety, but not when we feel ourselves actually in danger from them. 'We readily call these objects sublime, because they raise the forces of the soul above the height of vulgar commonplace, and discover within us a power of resistance of quite another kind, which gives us courage to be able to measure ourselves against the seeming omnipotence of nature' (KU v 261). This aspect of the sublime exalts our ability to rise above our fear of death, injury, and pain at the hands of nature; that is to say, we can in this respect regard ourselves as being above nature even though, in another, purely physical, aspect of our being, we are subject to it. Kant compares the feeling of this sublimity with the way in which the righteous man fears God, even though he believes that he himself, as a righteous man, has nothing to be afraid of; he still recognizes God as a being to be feared by anyone who transgresses his laws. Kant adds that the moral law, when considered from an aesthetic point of view, is sublime rather than beautiful; reverence or respect is the appropriate feeling for it, not love.

Kant says little about sublimity in works of art, not because he thinks it does not exist, but because it does not appear in a pure form, suitable for exhibition in a *Critique*, in any work or object which involves the notion of a definite end or purpose; in such cases, teleological considerations inevitably adulterate the purity of the aesthetic judgement. With the sublime as with the beautiful, Kant's aesthetics subordinates art to nature. In both cases, this is partly because the *Critique of Judgement* sets out primarily to provide a philosophy of organic nature, and partly because he believes that art is beautiful and great to the extent that it does in some sense follow or copy nature. This latter belief, however, is not argued in any thorough or comprehensive way, nor is it based on a thorough analysis of art as such; the *Critique* contains a number of *obiter dicta* about art in general and about various kinds or genres of art, but little systematic treatment of it.

Theoretically speaking, at least, we cannot say that natural objects are designed for a specific purpose, nor that the various parts or organs of a natural object or organism are designed to work to a specific end. To say this would be to imply that natural objects, so called, are not natural at all, but artificial. Kant makes use of teleological concepts in the interpretation of nature, but teleology in nature is for him an epistemological principle, not an objective, ontological one; in other words, the principle that nature is purposive belongs to the reflective, not the determinant, judgement. When we judge that the purpose of the heart is to circulate blood through the body, the concept of the purposiveness of nature is introduced to assist our reflection on the object under consideration, not to give it conceptual determination. It has a heuristic and investigatory value, but does not commit us to saying that this is how things really are; the purposiveness of the heart is to be contrasted with the actual, objective purpose or design of a watchmaker or an artist.

Thus when, for example, we say that the crystalline lens in the eye has the *purpose* of accomplishing by a second refraction of the light rays the focusing of those emanating from a point on the retina, all that is said is that the representation of a purpose in nature's causal action when creating an eye is to be thought because such an idea functions as a principle for conducting research concerning the lens of the eye, and likewise to help find the means which one might devise to expedite the result. In so doing, there is not attributed to nature a causality by the representation of ends—i.e. *intentional* action—which would be a determining teleological judgement, and as such a transcendent one since it instances a causality lying beyond the bounds of nature. (KU First Introduction xx 236.)

The physical sciences have some fundamental principles without which, as Kant argued in the first *Critique*, not merely would physics or natural science in general be impossible, but all experience also. The most important of these principles from the point of view of science is that every event has a cause or, as Kant sometimes rather misleadingly puts it, that nothing happens by chance. The main thesis of the teleological section of the *Critique of Judgement* is that the biological sciences have a basic principle of their own, which is often expressed in the maxim that nature does nothing in vain, but which Kant states more carefully as 'An organized natural product is one in which every part is reciprocally both end and means' (KU v 376). What this amounts to is that we cannot hope to understand the genesis and structure of plants and animals if we study them simply as the product of physical causal laws, i.e. as if they were mere machines. Of each part in the structure of an organism we must ask not merely 'How (i.e. as a result of what operations of mechanical causal laws) did this come to have the form it has?' but also 'What purpose does this part or organ serve in the operation of the whole?'; not merely, for example, 'As a result of what previous events does a tree in the spring come to develop leaves?' but also 'What do the leaves contribute to the life and growth of the tree?' The different parts of a natural organism contribute mutually to the life and activity of each other and of the organism as a whole. We may proceed, Kant thinks, to apply the same principle to nature considered as a whole; i.e. we may ask not merely 'What is the purpose of this or that particular natural object?' but also 'What is the purpose of nature considered as a whole?'

It is important not to misunderstand Kant's meaning here. He is not saying that everything in nature has, as a matter of fact, been designed by a mind or minds with certain purposes in view. As a convinced theist, he believes that this is so, but he is not arguing that the biological sciences have any theistic presuppositions; the existence of God and of actual design in nature are topics which belong to metaphysics, and no knowledge or proof concerning them can ever be achieved. He is saying, at this stage, merely that nature is unintelligible to us unless we regard it as if everything in it were purposively designed in the mutually helpful way he has described. The word 'mutually' needs to be stressed. Nature is not merely organized but self-organized; the existence of a watch logically presupposes the existence of a watchmaker, but the existence of nature does not logically presuppose the existence of a creator and designer of nature. The teleological principle of the natural sciences is, as we have seen, a regulative, not a constitutive, principle; it can be used as a maxim to guide us in our inquiries (indeed we must use it if our inquiries are to make any progress), but we must not assume that it is an objectively true proposition that nature is the result of design and does nothing in vain. The teleological principle is thus to be contrasted with the proposition that every event has a cause, which is objectively true of phenomena, even though it does not apply to things in themselves.

The behaviour of inorganic nature can be understood without the need of any teleological principle of explanation, while that of organic nature cannot. Nevertheless we may, according to Kant, treat inorganic natural phenomena as if they contributed towards a system of ends, even though we are not bound so to treat them.

Even products which do not . . . make it necessarily incumbent upon us to go beyond the mechanism of blind efficient causes and seek out some other principle on which they are possible, may nevertheless be justly estimated as forming part of a system of ends. For the idea from which we started is one which, when we consider its foundation, already leads beyond the world of sense, and then the unity of the supersensible principle must be treated, not as valid merely for certain species of natural objects, but as similarly valid for the whole of nature as a system. (KU v 380-1.)

In other words, although inorganic nature can be explained on mechanistic lines in terms of efficient causes, we can still ask teleological questions about it; we can ask 'What is the planetary system for?' even though we do not need to ask this question before we can understand the planetary system.

Just why, and in what respects, is the explanation of natural, purposive phenomena in terms of efficient causes inadequate? It might be thought that it was simply a matter of the relatively backward state of the biological, as opposed to the physical, sciences, and that with the passage of time this deficiency might be removed. It is, after all, always rash to put limits to the possibility of scientific discovery; granted that teleological explanations may be necessary until ordinary causal ones are available, is there any reason in principle why the former should not in the end be dispensed with by scientists, no matter how convenient it might be to retain the language of purpose in ordinary discourse? It is convenient for us to speak of the sun rising and setting, even if this is, scientifically speaking, a loose description of what actually happens; and it might still be convenient for us to say that it is the purpose or function of the heart to circulate blood through the body even if, eventually, the physiologist will want to express the same truth more accurately without using the language of purpose.

Now Kant would have disagreed strongly with this line of thought, but this by itself would not disprove the thesis; it would not be the first time that a philosopher had mistaken a temporary phenomenon for a universal law (not even, perhaps, the first time Kant himself had made this mistake). However, Kant's own detailed explanation of his position, difficult though it is to grasp its exact meaning, makes it clear that he is referring to permanent features of the human intellect; it is absurd, he insists, to hope that some second Newton might one day be found to explain the genesis of a blade of grass in terms of mechanical, non-teleological laws alone. In one of his earliest works, an essay entitled *Universal Natural History and Theory of the Heavens*, published in 1755, Kant had indeed seemed to leave open the possibility that the difficulty might one day be overcome, although he obviously thought that the day was far distant. There is no difficulty, he then claimed, in showing how the whole physical universe has come into its present state, given the general concept of matter and the force of attraction; his own attempt to do this is sometimes thought of as an anticipation of Laplace's nebular hypothesis of the origin of the solar system, though it is more metaphysical than scientific. But we are not, he added, in a corresponding position as far as the origin of animate nature is concerned. We cannot, from the general concept of matter and its laws of attraction, explain how even so simple a thing as a caterpillar could originate. By the time of the *Critique of Judgement*, thirty-five years later, Kant's explanation of the situation is different; in the intervening years his concentration on the analysis of the powers of the human mind as a preliminary to the establishment of metaphysical truth (or to the proof that such truths cannot be established) has led him to conclude that there is a fundamental and permanent difference between the physical and the biological sciences which is due to a fundamental and permanent feature of the human intellect. Kant tries to elucidate his position by giving another, and perhaps simpler, example of the way in which apparently objective logical or metaphysical truths are really dependent on subjective truths about the human mind. Take the distinction between the possibility and the actuality of things; the fact that we cannot avoid making the distinction and holding that some possible objects actually exist while others, equally possible, do not, is explained by the nature of our cognitive faculties, and in particular by the fact that our intellects have to work discursively, all our knowledge of objects requiring both concepts (derived from the understanding) and intuitions (derived from sensibility). The distinction between actuality and possibility can be made only because of the division of our intellectual functions between understanding and sensibility. From reflection on a concept we can deduce that an object instantiating it is possible (i.e. that it is not self-contradictory that an object answering to a given description should exist); but, contrary to what Descartes, Leibniz, and their followers may have thought, no amount of reflection on a concept can lead us to knowledge of whether there are actually objects answering to the concept—for this we need intuition, sensuous intuition in the case of empirical objects, pure intuition in the case of mathematical objects. There might conceivably exist a being or beings whose intellect was not limited in this way; beings who possessed an intuitive understanding or an intellectual intuition, i.e. whose knowledge was achieved, in some way unintelligible to us, directly and simply, not through the co-operation, so to speak, of our ability to construct concepts and of our ability to receive impressions through our senses. For such a being the distinction between actuality and possibility would not arise.

Again, in the practical sphere, the recognition that an action is prescribed by the moral law of reason is not, for human beings, necessarily enough to ensure the performance of that action; this also, Kant holds, is the result of a specifically human limitation, viz. the existence in men of a sensuous side of their nature. If there are any rational beings who are not limited in this way, then for them to recognize something as a law is to will accordingly, and there is no difference or gap between duty or obligation on the one hand and the corresponding action or volition on the other. Human beings, existing as they do under limitations imposed by their sensuous nature and by their existence in space and time, apprehend the moral law as embodying a command which they must obey even if they do not wish to do so.

Similarly, Kant says, were it not for the special conditions of our human intellects, we should find no distinction between mechanical and teleological principles of causal explanation. Our intellect has to move from the universal to the particular; we take a concept (that of a house, to take a simple empirical example) and judge that a particular which is given to us in sense-perception falls under it. We judge that the object in front of our eyes is a house, and the concept and the intuition are brought together by the power of judgement. The particular cannot be determined by, or derived from, the universal alone; for an empirical concept is an abstraction and includes only the properties common to all houses (say), so that any individual house will have many properties which are not contained in the concept. We can deduce some things about an object from the mere knowledge that it is a house, but an enormous number of its properties will be contingent; from the concept of a house we cannot tell how many rooms or windows or stories any particular house may have.

Now if we seek to discover the cause of a particular house's existence (and thus of its having the properties it has), there is no difficulty in seeing that we must refer to actual intention and design; part, at least, of its origin lies in the fact that it has been designed to have the form it has for a particular purpose or set of purposes. And if we seek to discover the cause of some phenomenon of inanimate nature (the tides, for example), we can be sure that an account of this will be possible without going beyond the principles of mechanical, physical causality (the tides behave as they do as a result of the gravitational pull of the moon and sun, whose motion again can be explained in a similarly non-teleological way). We can fully understand physical phenomena of this kind without ever asking the question 'What are these phenomena for?' or 'What purpose do they serve?' (This does not prevent us, if we wish, from believing that the physical universe has been created for a purpose; Kant's point is that such a belief adds nothing to our scientific understanding of the universe, and belongs to theology, not to physics.)

It is with attempts to discover the causes of natural products in animate nature that we find ourselves in an intermediate position. We cannot say, as we could in the case of the house, that it is a necessary condition of the existence of the natural product that the thought by some being of its existence should have formed part of the causal process which brought it into being; yet in our investigation of its origin we cannot help making use of the notion of a final cause. The biologist can attain only a partial understanding of the working of the human or canine heart, or of the human or canine body in general, so long as he sticks to mechanical causation alone. He must ask 'What is this for?' in order to gain full scientific understanding; it is not enough, as it was for the physicist, to ask 'How did this come about?', or rather, he cannot answer the latter question without first answering the former.

Teleology, thus exhibited, is neither a branch of theology nor a branch of natural science. It is not part of theology, for it does not assert anything about the objective existence and attributes of an author of nature as the cause or ground of natural phenomena; 'it only points to this cause in the interests of the reflective judgement engaged in surveying nature, its purpose being to guide our estimate of the things in the world by means of the idea of such a ground, as a regulative principle, in a manner adapted to our human understanding' (KU v 416). Similarly, it is not part of natural science; for the giving of objective causal explanations of natural phenomena cannot be the function of a merely reflective judgement, which is all that this form of teleology involves—natural science pursues, and to a certain extent achieves, the discovery of efficient, not final, causes. The science of teleology is not a branch of knowledge or doctrine but a branch of critical philosophy, and of the critique of the power of judgement in particular. Yet because the critique of judgement contains a priori principles, its findings have some relevance both for natural science and for theology, in spite of the fact that it does not belong to either of them.

Its relevance to natural science has already been discussed; the concluding pages of the *Critique of Judgement* discuss theological implications. Negatively, Kant's insistence on the distinction between purposiveness and design, and on the consequential distinction between the concept of teleology as applied to nature and the notion of a divine creation and organization of the universe, implies that any version of the argument from design is invalid. We cannot argue from the existence in nature of phenomena which present analogies or affinities with the products of human design and intention to the existence of any divine design or intention as the cause of those phenomena; and we cannot argue from the existence in nature of certain necessary conditions of human life and well-being to the existence of any wisdom or benevolence in the provision of those conditions. Kant always respects arguments of this sort—they spring as a rule, he thinks, from admirable motives and they can have a valuable persuasive effect on ordinary human beings—but, however persuasive they may be, they are not logically valid. His principal objection to these arguments is that they are all empirical; and arguments drawn from sense-experience can never entail conclusions which refer to something totally beyond, not merely all actual, but any possible, sense-experience. (The transcendence of God is admitted, if not insisted upon, by most advocates of this group of arguments for His existence.) Moreover, the argument includes an invalid step from part to whole; even if we allowed empirical premises to lead to transcendent conclusions, it is wrong to conclude from apparent signs of intention in part of nature to a divine design in the whole of nature, and equally wrong to conclude from apparent signs of wisdom or benevolence in some of the workings of nature to the existence of a perfectly wise and absolutely benevolent creator. There are, after all, many things in nature that do not look as if they were the result of design, and many more whose origin does not appear, prima facie at least, to exhibit wisdom or benevolence; we may be able to explain these things away consistently with a theology which includes divine creation together with omnipotence, omniscience, and absolute wisdom and benevolence in its doctrines, but a purely empirical approach cannot provide, or help to provide, such an explanation.

The application of teleological considerations to nature does, however, have some value for theology once the existence and attributes of God have been adequately determined in some other way. Once the existence of God has been established as a postulate of practical reason and thus as a presupposition of any genuine morality, this doctrine, together with the notion of man as a being whose capacity for morality is a function of his rationality, can give force and strength to the hypothetical reading of purpose into nature which is all that the *Critique of Judgement* by itself can establish. Once again it is the function of a Kantian *Critique* to deny knowledge in order to make room for faith: not to establish metaphysical knowledge by theoretical argument (in this case, knowledge that the whole of nature has been created by a wise and benevolent God in order to serve human needs and purposes) but, by showing that such an hypothesis at least makes sense as a heuristic device, to demonstrate that there is nothing contradictory or otherwise intellectually impossible in the notion of the divine nature and activity which is suggested by it, and consequently to allow us to make use of the concept of teleology to supplement the rational faith in God which the *Critique of Practical Reason* had justified. The essential point here is the status of man in nature. We can

E

think of many features in nature as serving as means to the activity and well-being of living things and creatures of various kinds; but so long as we leave mankind out of consideration we cannot, in Kant's view, explain why (that is, for what purpose) nature should have been created at all. Plants and animals can have only the purpose and functions with which they have been endowed by nature: the purpose of nature itself, therefore, cannot be simply to fulfil the purposes of plants and animals, to create conditions necessary for their survival and development. Even when we consider mankind as a possible ultimate end of creation, we cannot accept as a final determining ground a mere divine benevolence which wishes to make men happy, and has created nature in all its manifold variety to achieve this end; for why *should* man, considered merely as the most intelligent of the animals, be happy, and what worth or value could such happiness have from the point of view of nature or its creator? Man and his needs and purposes can form the ultimate end of nature only because he, unlike all other natural beings, can form his own ends, designs, or purposes—because, to use language drawn from the second *Critique*, man is the only being in nature who possesses autonomy of the will, and because, in particular, man can and indeed, morally speaking, must, set before himself as his ultimate objective the *summum bonum*, the achievement of the supreme moral good. For any other species of natural object or being, we can legitimately ask 'For what purpose does this object or being, plant or animal, exist?' We may not always be able to discover the answer; but unless the principle (which Kant claims to have shown must be adopted as a working hypothesis) that everything in nature is purposefully organized is in the end untrue, any answer that we can discover will eventually display a connexion between the existence of this particular species and some need or purpose of human beings. The connexion may of course be indirect, but unless it can be established we can see no rational justification for the existence of the species in question. (One possible way of establishing the connexion is suggested by Kant, though he does not insist that it is necessarily always the right way: we might say that the vegetable kingdom exists to serve the needs and purposes of herbivorous animals, who could not otherwise live; the herbivora exist to serve the needs of carnivora; and the whole structure of plant and animal life exists to serve mankind.)

We have in the world beings of but one kind whose causality is teleological, or directed to ends, and which at the same time are beings of such a character that the law according to which they have to determine ends for themselves is represented by themselves as unconditioned and not dependent on anything in nature, but as necessary in itself. The being of this kind is man, but man regarded as noumenon. He is the only natural creature whose peculiar objective characterization is nevertheless such as to enable us to recognize in him a supersensible faculty—his *freedom*—and to perceive both the law of the causality and the object of freedom which that faculty is able to set before itself as the highest end —the supreme good in the world. (KU v 435.)

Because of this, we cannot ask of man, as we can of all other natural beings, 'For what end or purpose does he exist?' He is an unconditioned end in himself, in virtue of his ability, as a rational, moral being, to legislate for himself and to act freely out of respect for the law which he thus imposes on himself. 'Only in man, and only in him as the individual being to whom the moral law applies, do we find unconditional legislation in respect of ends. This legislation, therefore, is what alone qualifies him to be a final end to which the whole of nature is teleologically subordinated' (KU v 436).

Kant may perhaps be criticized for making an over-eager transition from teleological talk about organisms in nature to teleological talk about nature as a whole. It may be difficult to discover any fully satisfactory way of describing and explaining the physiology of the human body without saying such things as 'The heart has the purpose, or function, of circulating the blood through the body'. If we omit all such words as 'function' and 'purpose', and say merely that the blood circulates as a result of the pumping of the heart, we are leaving out any mention of the fact that this circulation is a necessary condition of the successful working of the organism as a whole. But it is much easier to give meaningful descriptions of the behaviour of different species of plants or animals (even including reference to ways in which, as a result of the behaviour of one species, another species, which would otherwise have died, is enabled to live) without using teleological language. Indeed, one may say that, while it may, for some purposes, be a useful analogy to think of organisms in nature as if they were large-scale organs in a large-scale organism, this can only be an analogy; strictly speaking, nature is not an organism, and plants, animals, and men are not organs. And once one has pointed out that it is at best only a useful analogy, doubts may begin to arise about its usefulness.

Moreover, it might be held that Kant's insistence that our human intellects must regard nature throughout as a teleological system if we are to understand it is rendered less persuasive by the Darwinian doctrine of evolution through natural selection. The difficulty here is not the notion of evolution itself, which was enjoying something of a vogue when Kant wrote the *Critique of Judgement*; and Kant himself admits that new species might arise from old ones as a result of a mechanical causal process (cf. KU v 419). But if certain species have survived because they were of a sort to be able to take advantage of their natural environment in a way which their less successful and non-surviving rival species did not, we are surely not entitled to speak of the purposiveness of nature in providing the necessary conditions for their survival. If we have a set of natural conditions in which a number of different species live, and if some of those species are 'adapted' to survive in those conditions and others are not, we cannot speak of purpose unless we can suppose that it was part of some 'purpose of nature' that the species which survived should survive and that those which did not survive should not. But what grounds could there be for saying this? What ground could there be for the non-survival of the dinosaur except that it was unable to survive, natural conditions being what they were?

However, criticism of this kind applies with more force, perhaps, to some of Kant's *obiter dicta* about nature than to his strictly philosophical theses about it. All that he claims to have proved is that in examining nature we must, because of the inescapable limitations of our human intellects, make use of the concept of purposiveness. Whatever he may himself believe as a matter of faith, he does not claim to have proved the existence of actual, objective design or plan, either in the working of any particular organism, or in the ways in which different natural phenomena help to provide conditions necessary for the life and well-being of living creatures and, in particular, of men. Since Kant always had a simple, straightforward faith in the wisdom and benevolence of the author of nature, he sometimes gives the impression that his beliefs, which he held as a matter of faith, had been given more solid philosophical support from his critical writings than was actually the case. At his most careful, however, he does not make this mistake, but holds merely that the critical arguments show that the faith is not in itself contradictory or absurd.

# Conclusion

THE MIND OF A GREAT THINKER, contrary to what is sometimes suggested by historians who are interested in sources and origins, is not simply the resultant of a number of forces operating upon it; no matter how carefully and thoroughly one studies the way in which he has been influenced by his early education, by the work of previous or contemporary thinkers, by the social and political conditions of his own times, or by reflection on the history of past events, one will never by this means arrive at more than a superficial understanding and explanation of his thought. On the other hand, no thinker, however great, can escape such influences altogether. A philosopher will ask the questions he does because he believes either that, though important, they have not been asked before or that, although they have been asked by predecessors or contemporaries, they have as yet received no satisfactory answer; and his answers, however original, will preserve some echoes, conscious and unconscious, from his acquaintance with the thought of others.

Kant's general attitude to philosophy follows in many respects the main principles of the movement of thought known as the Enlightenment, especially in its German form. The principle that men should seek as far as possible to find systematically rational solutions to their problems, instead of relying on revelation, tradition, and the like, received its main philosophical support in Germany from Leibniz and his successors, especially Christian Wolff, and more practical support and encouragement from Frederick the Great. The principle was one which Kant earnestly professed and constantly observed, even though his use of reason led him in the end to conclusions which went far beyond those of his contemporaries and immediate predecessors. Some remarks in his essay *What is Enlightenment?* (published in 1784) provide a clear illustration of this attitude. Enlightenment, he explains, consists in a kind of liberation, in man's release from a tutelage or subjection which he has brought on himself.

Tutelage is man's inability to make use of his understanding without direction from another. This tutelage is self-incurred when its cause lies not in lack of reason but in lack of resolution and courage to use it without direction from another. *Sapere aude!* 'Have courage to use your own reason'—that is the motto of the Enlightenment—

and, one might add, Kant's own (VIII 36).

But this rather cold rationality was supplemented and transformed, especially in Kant's moral and political thinking, by two other factors. First in order of time was his exposure to the influence of the religious movement known as Pietism. This movement, to which his parents belonged and around which his early education was centred, represented an attempt to return to what was thought of as the true Protestant spirit of the Reformation—to a religion in which the individual soul, not the organized church, was all-important, and in which a sense of personal duty and discipline went with a distrust for external religious forms and observances. Kant accepted much of the more negative aspect of this attitude to religion, and never ceased to regard the pietists with great respect, even though they were far too dogmatic and irrationalist in their faith to satisfy him completely. Secondly, there was Rousseau, the reading of whose works in the 1760s, on Kant's own confession, corrected his growing tendency to value intellectual powers more highly than straightforward moral goodness, and encouraged him to search for a moral philosophy which should be based on reason but which should at the same time show how the ordinary unphilosophical man could understand, as well as perform, his duties—a philosophy which should not display any of the condescension so often shown, before and since, by philosophers to their supposed intellectual inferiors. More specifically, Kant derived from Rousseau his picture of human nature as distinguished from the rest of the animal creation, not by man's possession of an intellect but by his possession of freedom, in the sense of the capacity to pursue ends and objectives which he has spontaneously set before himself (animals being limited to the pursuit of ends given them by nature).

In a more narrowly philosophical context, Kant derived from Leibniz and his followers a belief in system as the distinguishing feature of philosophy. The essence of any scientific body of knowledge consists in the fact that it is systematic; common or unscientific knowledge is a mere aggregate of facts. His own philosophical system or 'architectonic', which has struck many commentators as artificial and valueless, is seen by Kant as providing a basis for philosophical certainty and the resolution of controversy, which he sees as the great scandal of philosophy;

the scientific, systematic, and critical investigation of philosophical problems, and especially of the nature and limitations of the human mind, replaces the existing state of war by a state of law and order (cf. KRV A751-2 B779-80). And Kant derived from Hume, as he tells us more than once, the impetus for his dissatisfaction with the dogmatic certainties of his philosophical predecessors and contemporaries, and his attempt to resurvey the foundations of the whole philosophical and metaphysical enterprise; from Hume's account of causation came also some hints, at least, towards the Kantian description and deduction of all the categories of the understanding, including that of cause and effect.

These influences, nevertheless, would have come to nothing without the integrating and originating power of Kant's own philosophical intellect. To see the need for a synthesis of all that is best in the outlook of the Enlightenment and all that is best in the thought of Rousseau is one thing: to devise a conceptual system and a philosophical method by means of which the synthesis could be provided is quite another. And while it is easy to say that a body of thought is philosophical only to the extent that it is systematic, the construction of an elaborate and profound system cemented together by acute and lengthy arguments is the most difficult of all philosophical enterprises. Kant, rightly, thought of his philosophy as revolutionary; and the originality of his achievement is emphasized by his often quoted, but sometimes misunderstood, comparison of himself to Copernicus. In the Preface to the second edition of the *Critique of Pure Reason* (KRV Bxvi-xvii) Kant says that Copernicus, having failed to find a satisfactory explanation of the movements of the heavenly bodies on the traditional supposition that they revolved round a stationary spectator, put forward the suggestion that the spectator revolves and the stars remain at rest. Kant makes an analogous suggestion in respect of metaphysics, viz. that objects, if they are to be known by us, must conform to our intuitions and concepts (i.e. to the conditions prescribed by the nature of human sensibility and understanding), instead of our intuitions and concepts having to conform to objects. On this latter view (universally held up to now) all a priori knowledge of objects would be impossible. The hypothesis of Copernicus was eventually vindicated by Newton: his own 'Copernican' hypothesis, Kant thinks, is vindicated by the arguments of the *Critique of Pure Reason.* It was by the truth or falsehood of this hypothesis and by the success or failure of its demonstration and application in the three *Critiques* and the other major works of the 1780s and 1790s that Kant's philosophical achievement was, in his own judgement, to be assessed. If we accept this judgement, we can hardly regard the critical philosophy as a complete success. Apart from actual mistakes and errors, some of which at least are relatively unimportant and could easily be corrected, it is now clear that Kant was unable in some respects to escape from the assumptions and prejudices of his own day. He takes for granted many positions and attitudes which seemed obviously correct to his contemporaries as well as to himself, but which subsequent thought and practice has shown to be partially, at least, open to question. In the first *Critique* he assumes without hesitation that Aristotelian logic, Euclidean geometry, and Newtonian physics are in essence the last word on their respective subjects; in the second he takes for granted that duty, considered as a sort of command or law, must be the central notion of human ethics, and accepts uncritically the eighteenth-century belief in an unchanging human nature; in the third, he takes for granted that the notions of the beautiful and the sublime comprise the entire field of aesthetics, and seems also to assume without question that art is the imitation of nature. To complain that Kant takes some things for granted is, of course, to complain that he is subject to ordinary human limitations; in reality no philosopher of science, morality, or art can possibly be sure that he has taken account in his philosophy not only of all past and present manifestations of science, morality, or art but of all future ones as well. One may have a right to complain of the over-optimistic tone of some of Kant's claims for the comprehensiveness and completeness of his philosophy; but in spite of this, it is doubtful whether, with the possible exception of Aristotle's, there has ever been a more comprehensive one.

In any case, a philosopher is not in the end to be judged entirely (perhaps not even at all) by the number and importance of his philosophical theses which appear to later generations still to be true. He is to be judged by the originality and range of his thought, by the depth and clarity of his arguments, and by his fecundity as a source of ideas for later thinkers. By these and by any other reasonable standards, Kant is worthy of a place among the very greatest philosophers.

# Recommended Reading

(I HAVE RESTRICTED my recommendations to works available in English.)

*General works*

N. Kemp Smith: *A Commentary to Kant's 'Critique of Pure Reason'* (2nd edn., London, 1923). Kemp Smith's views are at times coloured, not to say distorted, by his readiness to accept the view of the first *Critique* as a patchwork formed from sets of notes on different topics written at different times from different points of view and more or less haphazardly arranged. He is often too ready to find confusion and error in Kant, and to use supposed inconsistencies as evidence that the inconsistent parts of the work were composed at different times. But his commentary contains much valuable historical material that cannot readily be found elsewhere.

A. C. Ewing: *A Short Commentary on Kant's Critique of Pure Reason* (London, 1938). A short but sensible and helpful guide.

H. J. Paton: *Kant's Metaphysic of Experience* (2 vols., London, 1936). A long and detailed commentary on the first half of the *Critique of Pure Reason*; a work of great value to the advanced student.

H. J. Paton: *The Categorical Imperative: A Study in Kant's Moral Philosophy* (London, 1947). Primarily a commentary on the *Grundlegung*.

L. W. Beck: *A Commentary on Kant's Critique of Practical Reason* (Chicago, 1960). One of the best Kant commentaries ever written.

H. W. Cassirer: *A Commentary on Kant's Critique of Judgment* (London, 1938).

Mary J. Gregor: *Laws of Freedom* (A Study of Kant's Method of Applying the Categorical Imperative in the *Metaphysik der Sitten*) (Oxford, 1963).

S. Körner: *Kant* (Harmondsworth, 1955). A useful introductory guide.

J. Bennett: *Kant's Analytic* (Cambridge, 1966).

There is no fully recommendable biography of Kant in English; the biographical notes in F. Paulsen: *Immanuel Kant: His Life and Doctrine* (translated by J. E. Creighton and A. Lefevre, London, 1902) are still probably the best available. W. H. Bruford's *Germany in the Eighteenth Century* (Cambridge, 1935) gives an admirably clear picture of the social and political background.

*Some useful books on specific topics*

L. W. Beck: *Studies in the Philosophy of Kant* (Indianapolis, 1965). A most valuable collection of essays by one of the world's leading Kant scholars.

G. H. Bird: *Kant's Theory of Knowledge* (London, 1962).

E. Cassirer: 'Kant and Rousseau' (in *Rousseau-Kant-Goethe*, Princeton, 1947).

G. Martin: *Kant's Metaphysics and Theory of Science* (translated by P. G. Lucas, Manchester, 1955).

P. A. Schilpp: *Kant's Pre-Critical Ethics* (2nd edn., Evanston, 1960).

P. F. Strawson: *The Bounds of Sense* (London, 1966).

H.-J. de Vleeschauwer: *The Development of Kantian Thought* (translated by A. R. C. Duncan, London, 1962).

R. P. Wolff: *Kant's Theory of Mental Activity* (Cambridge, Mass., 1963).

Suggestions for further reading may be found in two surveys of recent Kant literature:

W. H. Walsh: 'Philosophical Survey: Kant', *Philosophical Quarterly* 3 (1953), 257.

M. J. Scott-Taggart: 'Recent Work on the Philosophy of Kant', *American Philosophical Quarterly* 3 (1966), 171.

The following articles, though not specifically about Kant, discuss in an interesting way topics with which he was concerned:

W. V. O. Quine: 'Two Dogmas of Empiricism', *Philosophical Review* 60 (1951), 20 (reprinted in *From a Logical Point of View* (Harvard, 1953), 20).

H. P. Grice and P. F. Strawson: 'In Defence of a Dogma', *Philosophical Review* 65 (1956), 141.

A. Quinton: 'Spaces and Times', *Philosophy* 37 (1962), 130.

G. Ryle: 'Categories', *Proceedings of the Aristotelian Society* 38 (1937-8), 189.

G. E. Moore: 'Is Existence a Predicate?', *Proceedings of the Aristotelian Society*, Supplementary Volume 15 (1936), 175 (reprinted in *Philosophical Papers* (London, 1959), 115).

T. Penelhum: 'Divine Necessity', *Mind* 69 (1960), 175.

D. Emmet: 'Universalisability and Moral Judgment', *Philosophical Quarterly* 13 (1963), 214.

R. M. Hare: 'Universalisability', *Proceedings of the Aristotelian Society* 55 (1954-5), 295.

# Index of Subjects

# Index of Names